SPLENDID ISOLATION

ART OF EASTER ISLAND

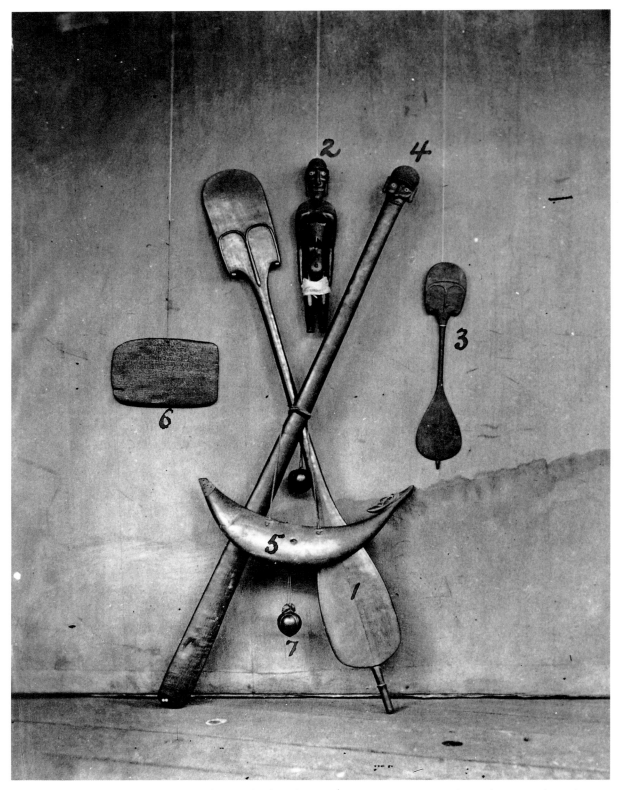

Photograph of Rapa Nui works from the collection of Bishop Florentin Étienne "Tepano" Jaussen, late 19th century. The works include: (1) a large dance paddle (*'ao*); (2) wood figure (*moai tangata*); (3) dance paddle (*rapa*); (4) chief's staff (*ua*); (5) gorget (*rei miro*); (6) inscribed tablet (*kohau rongorongo*); and (7) two *tahonga*. National Anthropological Archives, Smithsonian Institution, Washington, D.C.

SPLENDID ISOLATION

ART OF EASTER ISLAND

ERIC KJELLGREN

With contributions by Jo Anne Van Tilburg and Adrienne L. Kaeppler

The Metropolitan Museum of Art, New York

Yale University Press, New Haven and London

This volume is published in conjunction with the exhibition "Splendid Isolation: Art of Easter Island," held at The Metropolitan Museum of Art, New York, from December 11, 2001, to August 4, 2002.

The exhibition is made possible by Compañía Sud Americana de Vapores and Viña Santa Rita.

The exhibition catalogue is made possible, in part, by the Mary C. and James W. Fosburgh Publications Fund.

Published by The Metropolitan Museum of Art, New York

John P. O'Neill, Editor in Chief
Dale Tucker, Editor
Robert Weisberg, Designer
Megan Arney, Production Manager
Map designed by Anandaroop Roy

Color separations by Professional Graphics, Inc., Rockford, Illinois
Printed and bound by Meridian Printing, East Greenwich, Rhode Island

Cover: Male figure (*moai tangata*). The Metropolitan Museum of Art (cat. no. 13)

Library of Congress Cataloging-in-Publication Data

Kjellgren, Eric.
    Splendid isolation : art of Easter Island/by Eric Kjellgren with contributions by Jo Anne Van Tilburg and Adrienne L. Kaeppler.
      p.   cm.
    Includes bibliographical references.
    ISBN 1-58839-011-X (pbk. : alk. paper) — ISBN 0-300-09078-1 (pbk. : alk. paper : Yale University Press)
    1. Antiquities, Prehistoric—Easter Island—Exhibitions. 2. Art—Easter Island—Exhibitions. 3. Easter Island—Antiquities—Exhibitions. I. Van Tilburg, Jo Anne. II. Kaeppler, Adrienne Lois. III. Title.

GN875.E17 K54 2001
732'.2'099618—dc21   2001044732

Contents

Sponsor's Statement

Compañía Sud Americana de Vapores S.A. and S.A. Viña Santa Rita are proud to sponsor this exhibition devoted to the art of Easter Island, a remote Chilean island located in the South Pacific.

Our sponsorship indicates our desire to bring the art of this fascinating island to a wide public through the exhibition of fifty works made of stone, wood, and other materials, and dating from the thirteenth to the late nineteenth century.

Our sponsorship also indicates that our companies are acting globally in supporting the first American exhibition of this intriguing art from a faraway island.

Ricardo Claro
Chairman
Compañía Sud Americana de Vapores S.A.
and
S.A. Viña Santa Rita

Director's Foreword

Perhaps no images in Oceanic art are as familiar and yet as enigmatic as the colossal, brooding stone figures of Easter Island. In many ways they are the quintessential symbols of Pacific Island art and culture. Easter Island's other artistic traditions, however, remain largely unfamiliar to wider audiences. "Splendid Isolation: Art of Easter Island" is the first American exhibition to survey a broad range of the island's art—from the towering stone figures to smaller, more refined works in wood, feathers, fiber, and barkcloth—revealing the true richness of artistic expression on this small Pacific island, one of the most remote inhabited places on earth.

As elsewhere in Polynesia, artists on Easter Island concentrated primarily on the creation of religious images—making visible the gods, spirits, and ancestors whose powers they believed controlled the human world. Some of the most accomplished of these images include the island's superbly crafted wood sculptures. These highly polished, subtly curved figures reflect both naturalistic and stylized conceptions of the human body as well as a variety of zoomorphic forms. Perhaps the most striking are the "birdmen," which portray the Rapa Nui creator god Makemake as a fantastic hybrid of human and bird. In their otherworldly blending of anthropomorphic and zoomorphic imagery, these figures appear at times almost Surrealistic. It comes as no surprise, then, that Rapa Nui wood sculpture was an important source of inspiration for a number of Surrealist painters, particularly Max Ernst, whose works often contain imagery inspired by Easter Island art.

The achievement of Easter Island artists is also evident in the island's diverse decorative arts. Created to adorn the bodies of chiefs and other prominent individuals, these works are intimate in scale. Although their forms and imagery were largely dictated by custom, each example can stand alone as a work of art, reflecting the idiosyncrasies of the master carver's hand and, perhaps, the individual taste of the wearer.

This exhibition features outstanding works from the Metropolitan's select collection of Easter Island sculpture, which encompasses the full history of the Museum's Oceanic collection—from a work donated by Gertrud A. Mellon in 1972 to the Museum of Primitive Art, the institutional predecessor of the Metropolitan's Department of the Arts of Africa, Oceania, and the Americas, to important bequests from Nelson A. Rockefeller in 1979 to a lizardman figure acquired in 1995. The depth and scope of the exhibition have been greatly enriched through the generosity of more than a dozen museums and private collectors in the United States and Canada, a number of whom graciously agreed to loan their most important Easter Island works for the first time. We thank them all for their vital contributions.

In the exhibition catalogue, Eric Kjellgren, Evelyn A. J. Hall and John A. Friede Assistant Curator of Oceanic Art in the Department of the Arts of Africa, Oceania, and the Americas, places Easter Island's artistic heritage within its historical and cultural context. Never losing sight of the works' remarkable aesthetic qualities, he surveys what is known, and unknown, about the island's diverse forms of artistic expression. Adrienne L. Kaeppler, Curator of Oceanic Ethnology at the National Museum of Natural History, Smithsonian Institution, and Jo Anne Van Tilburg of the Institute of Archaeology, University of California, Los Angeles, discuss the social contexts of the island's well-known stone figures as well as its less familiar religious and decorative arts. Together, the authors join with other contemporary Oceanic art scholars in the effort to dispel lingering misconceptions about the origins and nature of Easter Island art and to give rightful credit for the island's artistic achievement to its original Polynesian creators, the Rapa Nui.

For his organization of the exhibition and authorship of the catalogue, I express the Museum's particular appreciation to Eric Kjellgren. I also wish to thank Adrienne L. Kaeppler and Jo Anne Van Tilburg for their valuable contributions. The Metropolitan Museum extends its sincere thanks to the Compañía Sud Americana de Vapores S.A. and S.A. Viña Santa Rita for their generous support of the exhibition. We are also indebted to the Mary C. and James W. Fosburgh Publications Fund for its important contribution to the exhibition catalogue. To them and to all those within and beyond the Metropolitan who worked to make this exhibition possible, the Museum owes a debt of gratitude. In bringing one of Earth's most remote artistic traditions to the attention of a broader audience, they help to further the Metropolitan's ongoing commitment to encompass the full range and richness of human artistic achievement and present it to the world.

Philippe de Montebello
Director, The Metropolitan Museum of Art

Acknowledgments

This exhibition and catalogue would not have been possible without the generosity, guidance, and support of many individuals both within and beyond the walls of the Metropolitan Museum. I especially thank Adrienne L. Kaeppler and Jo Anne Van Tilburg not only for their own contributions to the catalogue but also for their careful reading of and comments on the introduction and catalogue entries and for their willingness to lend their enthusiasm and expertise to numerous aspects of the project. I also wish to express my deep gratitude to the Compañía Sud Americana de Vapores S.A. and S.A. Viña Santa Rita for their generous support of the exhibition.

Other museum colleagues outside the Metropolitan provided invaluable assistance to me in the preparations for the exhibition. I wish to thank in particular Deborah Hull-Walski, Felicia Pickering, and Susan Crawford, Department of Anthropology, Smithsonian Institution, Washington D.C.; Nynke Dorhout and Genevieve Fisher, Peabody Museum of Archaeology and Ethnology, Harvard University, Cambridge, Massachusetts; Paul Beelitz and Maria Yakimov, American Museum of Natural History, New York; Diane Pelrine and Anita Bracalente, Indiana University Art Museum, Bloomington; Andrea Kirkpatrick and Anne Marr, New Brunswick Museum, Saint John, Canada; Christina Hellmich and Lucy Butler, Peabody Essex Museum, Salem, Massachusetts; and John Pretola and Diane Waterhouse-Barbarisi, Springfield Science Museum, Massachusetts.

A number of individual lenders graciously agreed to part temporarily with some of their prized Easter Island objects. I want to express my particular gratitude to Mark and Carolyn Blackburn, Arman and Corice Arman, Faith-dorian Wright, Raymond and Laura Wielgus, and Francesco Pellizzi, who made available works from the Helios Trust Collection, as well as to those lenders who preferred to remain anonymous.

At the Metropolitan Museum, my thanks go first and foremost to Julie Jones, Curator in Charge of the Department of the Arts of Africa, Oceania, and the Americas, whose constant support and willingness to share the wisdom gained through many years of experience with all aspects of the exhibition process have been invaluable. I also want to thank Philippe de Montebello for his support of the exhibition. I am indebted to many of my departmental colleagues, in particular Heidi King, for her advice on the exhibition catalogue, Hillit Zwick, and Christine Giuntini, for her assistance with conservation and mount designs for the barkcloth figures and feather headdresses. I am also grateful to Ross Day, Leslie Lowe Preston, and Joy Garnett of the Robert Goldwater Library for helping me to track down many vital references on Easter Island art and culture.

Numerous individuals in other departments at the Metropolitan also provided vital assistance. I thank them all, especially: Dan Kershaw, Sophia Geronimus, and Zack Zanolli, Design Department; Lisa Cain, Registrar, who worked under the able supervision of Aileen Chuk; Leslie Gat and Ellen Howe, Objects Conservation, and their colleagues Nancy Reynolds, Alexandra Walcott, and Fred Sager, who made mounts for the objects; Sarah Higby and Rosayn Anderson, Development; and Naomi Takafuchi, Communications.

The devotion to excellence of the staff of the Editorial Department, under the guidance of John P. O'Neill, Editor in Chief, is evident in this publication. I want to thank particularly my editor, Dale Tucker, whose dedication and tireless efforts are reflected in the text. I am also deeply grateful to Peter Antony and, especially, to Megan Arney for the catalogue's production. Robert Weisberg provided the elegant catalogue design, and the map of Easter Island was created by Anandaroop Roy. I am greatly indebted to the Mary C. and James W. Fosburgh Publications Fund for its important contributions to the exhibition catalogue. In the Photograph Studio, I thank Karin L. Willis for her original photography of many of the objects and Mark Morosse for photographing the works by Max Ernst and Pierre Loti. I also want to express my gratitude to Colta Ives, Curator, Drawings and Prints, for helping me to locate and allowing me to include the work by Max Ernst. I express my heartfelt thanks to these individuals and to all those who contributed in both large and small ways to the success of this exhibition and catalogue.

Eric Kjellgren

SPLENDID ISOLATION

ART OF EASTER ISLAND

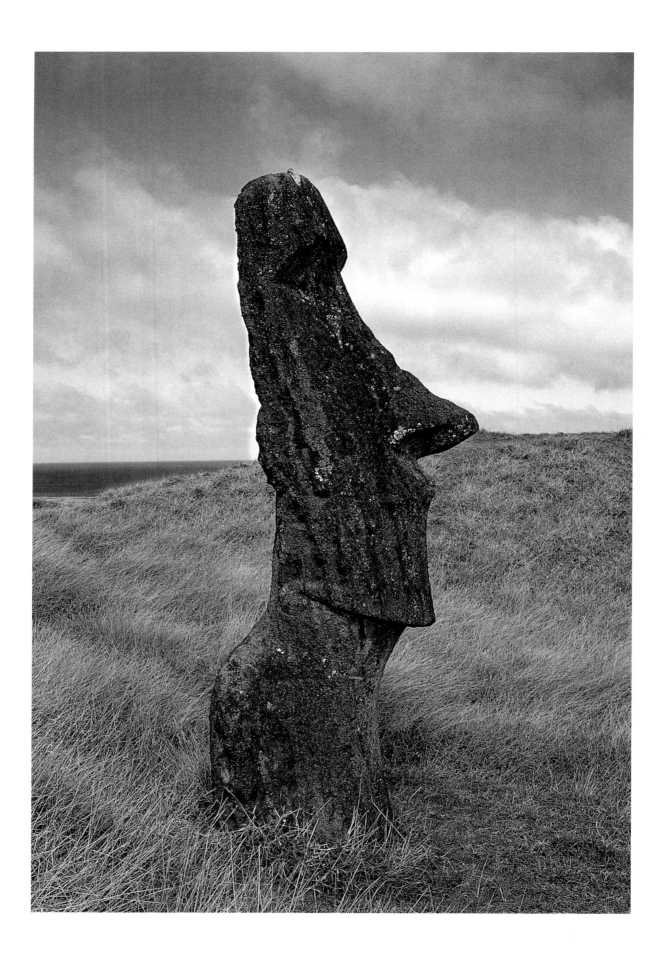

Introduction: Remote Possibilities

Eric Kjellgren

On Easter Sunday, 1722, an expedition under the command of Dutch navigator Jacob Roggeveen was exploring the vast expanse of the southeast Pacific when they sighted a small volcanic island. Although unaware of it at the time, they were probably the first vessels to touch at its shores in more than a thousand years. When a landing party went ashore the following day in search of water and provisions, they encountered an art and culture that had been developing in virtual isolation for centuries. The sailors marveled to see gigantic stone figures—some reaching heights of up to thirty feet and many crowned by massive cylinders of porous red rock—standing in silent rows along the shore. The presence of the colossal figures in this all but treeless land, whose inhabitants appeared to lack the means to create them, seemed an unfathomable mystery.

The Dutch left the island with little but the name they gave it—Paasch Eyland, or Easter Island. But for subsequent generations of explorers, as well as the missionaries, ethnographers, archaeologists, eccentrics, and travelers who followed, this small island and its colossal sculpture have inspired an unceasing fascination.[1] No other indigenous art in the Pacific has so captivated the Western imagination as that of Easter Island. Its immense stone figures, or *moai*, are for many the most familiar and recognizable sculptural tradition within Oceanic art, and they remain an enduring image in global popular culture (fig. 1).

Despite its renown, Easter Island's art has to date received little serious attention from art scholars and is seldom exhibited outside of ethnographic contexts. Although the island's carved wood figures enjoyed some popularity among European artists and intellectuals from the 1870s to the 1930s, today most of the island's artistic traditions remain virtually unknown outside a small group of specialists. In addition to stone, Easter Island artists worked in richly grained wood and other, more delicate materials such as feathers and a fine paperlike barkcloth obtained from the island's stunted trees. The supple curves and intricately decorated surfaces of these other art forms contrast with the robust angularity of the *moai*. Many are among the most accomplished works of Oceanic sculpture. A knowledge of their cultural significance enhances the experience of Easter Island's artistic traditions, but the works can also be appreciated on purely aesthetic grounds. It is time to recognize Easter Island not only as the home of one of the Pacific's most fascinating cultures but also for its unique contributions to Oceanic art.

As with other Oceanic artistic traditions, the objects and designs that Western scholars refer to collectively as Easter Island "art" were originally created for a variety of purposes and were perceived and classified by their

1. The area of Easter Island is 64 square miles (160 km²), or roughly twice the size of Manhattan.

Opposite: Figure 1. *Moai* on the exterior slope of the statue quarry at Rano Raraku.

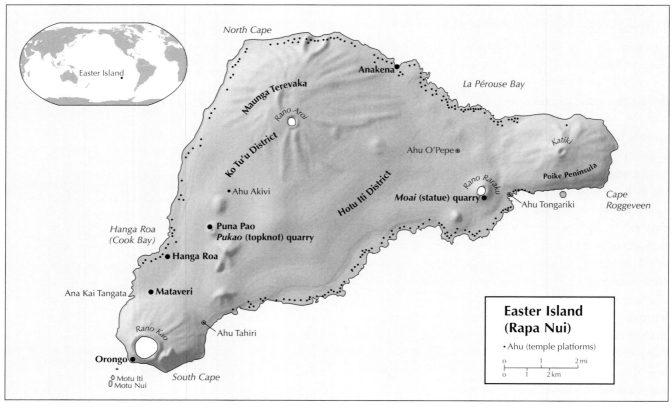

Figure 2. Map of Easter Island (Rapa Nui), showing principal sites and the placement of *ahu*.

Easter Island

Easter Island
(Rapa Nui)

• Ahu (temple platforms)

2. The name Rapa Nui, or Rapanui, is not recorded prior to the 1860s, and it is possible that no term for the island as a whole existed prior to European contact. As its older name, Easter Island, is more familiar, I have retained it when referring to the island and use Rapa Nui to refer to its people.
3. Although some, most famously the Norwegian archaeologist Thor Heyerdahl, posit a South American origin for the Rapa Nui, this contention is not supported by existing cultural, archaeological, linguistic, or genetic evidence, all of which indicate they are of East Polynesian ancestry.

creators in ways that differ markedly from the Western appreciation of them. Art on Easter Island embodied and signified *mana,* the supernatural power of the gods (*atua*) and of the chiefs (*ariki*) considered to be their descendants on earth. To harness this power, Easter Island carvers fashioned images of supernatural beings, ranging from the creator god, Makemake, a hybrid "birdman" being, to powerful ancestral chiefs and the dangerous, emaciated spirits of the dead. These images were used in a variety of contexts.

Since Roggeveen first described the *moai* nearly three centuries ago, Western observers have sought to understand the origins and significance of Easter Island sculpture. In the process, they have attributed the works to almost every culture on earth (and even a few beyond it) with the general exception of the one that actually created them. Although highly speculative theories persist, the origin of Easter Island's art has never been a mystery. The stone giants were erected not by a lost race but by the ancestors of the islanders whom Roggeveen encountered and whose descendants live on the island today.

In form, imagery, and function, Easter Island's art, like its people, language, and culture, is distinctively Polynesian. The Easter Islanders, who today refer to themselves and to their homeland as Rapa Nui,[2] are the easternmost of some thirty-six Polynesian peoples whose ancestors discovered and settled the islands of the central and eastern Pacific. Culturally and genetically, they share a common ancestry with other Polynesians, such as the Hawaiians, Tahitians, and the New Zealand Māori.[3]

The ancestors of the Polynesians began to migrate eastward from Island Southeast Asia about 1500 B.C.[4] Known as the Lapita culture, these early voyagers spread rapidly throughout the western Pacific, reaching the previously uninhabited archipelagoes of Fiji, Tonga, and Samoa by 1000 B.C. About the middle of the first millennium B.C. the descendants of Lapita settlers developed what are recognizably Polynesian cultures. Between 200 B.C. and A.D. 1, Polynesian navigators began to move farther eastward into the largely landless expanse of the eastern Pacific, likely settling first in the Cook and Marquesas Islands.

In terms of the epic scale and navigational precision of their voyages, the Polynesians were the most accomplished sailors in the ancient world. Guided only by the stars, the flight patterns of seabirds, and the form and rhythm of ocean swells, Polynesian navigators discovered and traveled between some of the most remote islands on earth and settled virtually every habitable island within the vast "Polynesian triangle," formed by New Zealand, Hawai'i, and Easter Island. These islands were settled not by chance encounter but by well-equipped colonizing expeditions employing large, double-hulled sailing canoes that carried people as well as the animals and crops necessary to establish permanent settlements. Sometime between A.D. 600 and 800, a group of colonists set out from an unidentified island in eastern Polynesia.[5] Heading southeast, they spent many weeks on open sea before at last sighting Easter Island.

That Easter Island was discovered at all is testimony to the skills of the Polynesian navigators. Even today, it remains one of the most remote inhabited places on earth. A triangular landmass formed by three extinct volcanoes, Easter Island lies more than a thousand miles from the islands of eastern Polynesia and some 1,400 miles from the South American coast (fig. 2). At 27 degrees south of the equator, Easter Island is outside the tropics, and adjusting to its cooler climate proved a challenge for the settlers, whose culture, crops, and domestic animals were adapted to tropical conditions. Archaeological evidence and surviving oral traditions suggest that Easter Island, although possibly discovered on an earlier voyage, was settled only once, by a single group of colonists whose descendants lived in virtual isolation for the next thousand years.

According to Rapa Nui accounts, the island was settled by Hotu Matu'a, a powerful chief who arrived with a party of colonists in two large sailing canoes.[6] The island that Hotu Matu'a and his followers found differed greatly from the grassy, treeless land described by the earliest European explorers. Analysis of fossil pollen and impressions of tree trunks preserved in lava flows indicate that Easter Island was originally covered by dense palm forests and stands of *toromiro* and other small trees.[7] Seabirds, sea turtles, and marine mammals visited its shores, but, with the possible exception of a single species of lizard, Easter Island originally had no land animals.[8]

To this new land the Polynesians brought their staple crops of taro, sugarcane, yams, sweet potatoes, and bananas, as well as the paper mulberry tree (*Broussonetia papyrifera*), whose inner bark was processed to create a fine white barkcloth used for garments and ritual effigies. While the settlers' canoes likely carried the four Polynesian domestic animals—the pig,

4. This description and chronology of Polynesian settlement are based on those of Kirch. Kirch 2000, pp. 207–45.

5. The closest inhabited island, Pitcairn, lies roughly 900 miles to the northwest of Easter Island. Its coast consists primarily of steep cliffs and lacks a good harbor, making Pitcairn an unlikely homeland for the settlers of Easter Island. Instead, Easter Island was probably colonized from an undetermined location in the Austral, Mangarevan, or Marquesas archipelagoes.

6. For an overview of the various versions of the Hotu Matu'a story, see Métraux 1940, pp. 55–69.

7. For a discussion of the paleo-botanical evidence for the island's forests, see Van Tilburg 1994, p. 47. The palm forests are generally thought to have been composed, in whole or in part, of the Chilean wine palm (*Jubaea chilensis*). Palm trees, likely used to construct the sleds or rollers on which the *moai* were moved, and *toromiro* (*Sophora toromiro*), the primary material for the wood images, proved crucial to the development of the island's art.

8. It is uncertain whether this lizard (*Cryptoblepharus boutonii*) represents an indigenous species or a later Polynesian introduction. Van Tilburg 1994, p. 48.

9. This account of Rapa Nui social organization is based on Van Tilburg 1994, pp. 86–93.
10. *Mata* literally translates as "eye" and is used by extension to designate the face or, more broadly, a group whose members share a common ancestor.
11. Hotu Matu'a's first son, Tuu-ma-heke, is said to have returned to the original homeland, leaving the second son, Miru, from whom the *mata* derives its name, as the island's spiritual and political leader. Van Tilburg 1994, p. 88.
12. Métraux 1940, p. 120.
13. Van Tilburg 1994, p. 88.
14. Kaeppler 1989, p. 212.

dog, chicken, and rat—only the latter two species survived. As a result, chickens assumed the ceremonial role played by pigs in other Polynesian societies, becoming the most valued and sacred animal for ritual feasts and offerings.

From the beginning, Rapa Nui society was organized following the classic Polynesian pattern, with an aristocracy composed of ranked hereditary chiefs (*ariki*) who held political authority over the common people (*hurumanu*), and a third, lower-ranking group (*kio*) comprising landless individuals and refugees.[9] Social status was based on primogeniture, with the eldest male child inheriting the bulk of the parents' supernatural and secular power. Rapa Nui society was essentially patriarchal, but *ariki* women also wielded considerable influence.

Politically, the Rapa Nui were divided into ten descent groups (*mata*), each of which traced its ancestry to one of the sons of Hotu Matu'a.[10] The highest-ranking *mata* was the Miru, the ruling aristocracy who descended from Hotu Matu'a's second son.[11] The island was partitioned into a number of separate, often mutually hostile, districts. Initially the districts might have been the homelands of the separate *mata*, but centuries of warfare and intermarriage resulted in at least some members of each *mata* living in each district.[12] Political authority rested with the local *ariki* as well as with *matatoa*, accomplished war leaders who could be of either chiefly or commoner ancestry.

The highest of the Miru chiefs was recognized by the entire population as the island's paramount chief (*ariki mau*). The most direct descendant of Hotu Matu'a and, ultimately, of the gods, the *ariki mau* embodied the supernatural power (*mana*) of the gods and was Easter Island's religious leader. The central figure at rites of increase and renewal and at other rituals, he worked with the gods to ensure the continuing fertility of the land and sea.[13] Although the *ariki mau* played an important role, most rituals were actually conducted by priests called *ivi atua* ("bones of the gods"), who were drawn from the nobility.

To mark the social ranks of *ariki, matatoa,* and other prominent individuals, many forms of Rapa Nui art, as in other Polynesian traditions, are devoted to what has been termed an "aesthetic of inequality."[14] High-ranking men and women wore distinctive regalia and wielded attributes of rank to mark their separate and exalted status. These included the bifacial chief's staffs (*ua*) carried by some male *ariki,* the graceful crescent-shaped *rei miro* pendants worn primarily by chiefly women, and *hau kurakura*, brightly colored headdresses made with highly prized red-orange rooster feathers and worn by Rapa Nui warriors.

The primary focus of Easter Island art, however, was on the creation of religious images. It is probable that the first settlers brought wood or stone figures with them. By historical times, a great diversity of images had developed, from wood objects that fit in the palm of the hand to an unfinished *moai* more than 70 feet high. Through art, Rapa Nui artists sought to make visible the gods, spirits, and ancestral chiefs whose powers could sustain or destroy the world. These figures and statuary acted as temporary or permanent containers and conduits for the *mana* of the beings they represented, serving as points of contact between humans and the divine.

Much of our knowledge of Rapa Nui religion and iconography remains fragmentary. Most sacred knowledge was transmitted orally; however, the Rapa Nui are unique among Polynesian peoples in their development and use of an indigenous script. Known as *rongorongo,* it consisted primarily of stylized anthropomorphic and zoomorphic symbols recorded on wood tablets (*kohau rongorongo*) and shorter inscriptions on figures and ornaments. Some scholars speculate that *rongorongo* is a postcontact development created in imitation of European writing, but the precise age and origins of the script have yet to be determined. Knowledge of *rongorongo* was restricted to specialized priests (*tangata rongorongo*), who gathered periodically to recite from the tablets. Once numerous, almost all *rongorongo* tablets were destroyed or allowed to decay following the adoption of Christianity in the late 1860s, and only about two dozen examples survive.[15] The inscriptions likely recorded myths, histories, and genealogies, but they have never been satisfactorily deciphered.

Surviving oral traditions and historical accounts indicate that Rapa Nui cosmology encompassed a variety of supernatural beings whose powers and spheres of influence ranged from the universal to the highly specific. These included the major and minor gods (*atua*) as well as lesser spirits known as *akuaku.* For much of Easter Island's history, however, its art and religion centered largely on the spirits of ancestral chiefs, and it is these ancient *ariki* who are represented in the colossal stone *moai.*

The identity of the *moai* was first documented in 1774 by the renowned English explorer Captain James Cook. Using a rudimentary vocabulary culled from several Polynesian languages and possibly assisted by Mahine, a Tahitian man who accompanied the expedition, the members of Cook's party were able to question the Rapa Nui about the meaning of the stone images.[16] In his journal, Cook recorded how the islanders described the *moai:*

> [They] give different names to them such as Gotomoara, Marapoti
> . . . Matta Matta &c to which the[y] some times prefix the word
> Moi [moai] and some times annex Areekee [ariki]: the latter signi-
> fies Chief and the other burying or sleeping place.[17]

Although Cook apparently confused the word *moai* (image) with *moe* (sleep), the crux of what the Rapa Nui said seems clear—the figures are *moai* (images) of *ariki* (chiefs), whose names Cook notes. In fact, Matta Matta, which Cook records as a proper name, may represent a mishearing of the term *mata mata* (faces). If so, the islanders were probably telling Cook's crew that the figures were *moai mata mata ariki,* or "images of the faces of chiefs."[18]

The *moai*—with their strictly symmetrical, somewhat rigid frontal orientation, enlarged heads, and arms extending down their sides to hands that rest on markedly convex stomachs—reflect the classical stylistic conventions of Polynesian figures. Although larger in scale than other eastern Polynesian sculpture, the general form of the *moai* exhibits close affinities with works from Tahiti, the Marquesas, and the Cook and Austral Islands.

Like other specialized activities, the carving of *moai* was performed by experts (*maori*), whose abilities were recognized within the community.[19]

15. Fischer 1997, pp. 403–508.
16. Polynesian languages are closely related, and Mahine, who spoke Tahitian, was able to communicate with many of the Polynesian peoples encountered by Cook's expedition. Forster 2000, p. 303. Whether Mahine played any role in obtaining information about the *moai* is unknown.
17. Beaglehole 1961, p. 359. Cook here summarizes information provided by several members of the expedition.
18. William J. Thomson recorded that the stone used to make most of the *moai* was called *maea matariki.* Thomson 1891, p. 452. This may be a contraction of *maea mata ariki,* or "stone [for making] the face of chiefs."
19. The term *maori* should not be confused with Māori, the indigenous people of New Zealand.

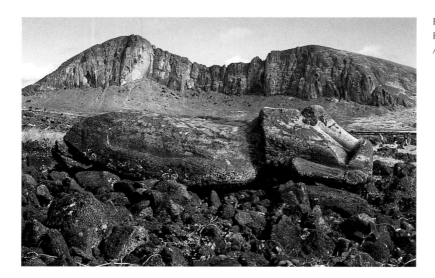

20. Van Tilburg 1994, p. 90.
21. Thomson 1891, p. 498;
Routledge 1919, pp. 183–84.
22. Van Tilburg 1992, pp. 86, 208.
23. Van Tilburg 1994, pp. 21–23.
24. Ibid., pp. 52, 67.

Each *moai* was fashioned by a group of expert stone carvers under the direction of a master sculptor (*tangata honui maori*), who was credited as the *moai*'s creator.[20] The names of these master carvers have been largely lost to history but appear to have been well known among their contemporaries and descendants. Late-nineteenth- and early-twentieth-century sources report that the Rapa Nui still recalled the identities of a number of *moai* carvers. One man proudly claimed descent from a *moai* carver named Unrautahui and another account asserts that the first *moai* was created by a sculptor named Tai-hare-atua.[21]

The earliest *moai* appear to have been carved about 1100 and the last in the mid-1600s, although precise dating remains tentative.[22] Nearly nine hundred were made, ranging from 8 feet in height to an unfinished example that is 71 feet, the average being just over 13 feet and weighing 8 to 10 metric tons.[23] All but a handful were carved from the soft volcanic tuff of Rano Raraku, a shallow volcanic crater that served as the primary statue quarry (fig. 3). Once completed, many *moai* were transported to the coast on wood sleds or rollers and erected on large temple platforms (*ahu*) made of earth and stone that had been built to receive them.

By the mid-sixteenth century, the island's population, originally perhaps a few dozen individuals, is believed to have peaked at about seven to nine thousand people.[24] This large population provided ample labor for the construction of *moai*, but it also increased pressure on the island's limited natural resources. The resulting environmental degradation is believed to have resulted in greater competition for raw materials and agricultural land. An increase in internecine warfare ensued in which war leaders (*matatoa*) assumed prominent positions. Secular authority, which had been held by the individual districts, became increasingly concentrated in a single, ritually determined, leader. These social changes, coupled with the eventual overharvesting and disappearance of the large trees needed to move and erect the massive stone sculptures, ultimately led to the demise of the *moai* tradition.

In its place, new ceremonies and art forms arose devoted primarily to the gods (*atua*) and to a diversity of spirits known collectively as *akuaku*.

Foremost among the *atua* was the creator god, Makemake. Born from a floating skull that was washed from a temple into the sea, Makemake created the first humans and, with his companion, the goddess Haua, brought the first flocks of migratory seabirds to the island.[25] As early as the fifteenth century a series of annual religious rites developed that were centered on Makemake, specifically in his manifestation as the *tangata manu,* or birdman.[26]

In contrast with the *moai* rites, which were widely dispersed throughout the island, the birdman religion focused primarily on a single ceremonial center known as Orongo. Perched atop the narrow outer rim of Rano Kau, an extinct volcano at the southwest corner of the island, Orongo is bounded on one side by the steep inner walls of the crater and on the other by sheer cliffs that descend a thousand feet to the sea.

The birdman rites took the form of a ritualized competition to determine political leadership of the island. Unlike the hereditary *ariki mau,* the position of the secular leader—known as the "birdman" (*tangata manu*)—was potentially open to any chief from the current ruling elite.[27] Although he was concerned mostly with secular affairs, the birdman was regarded as sacred and, possibly, as a living incarnation of Makemake. The birdman ceremonies climaxed in September, when *manu tara,* or sooty terns (*Sterna fuscata*), began to nest on Motu Nui, a tiny islet just offshore from Rano Kau (fig. 4). At this time four or more chiefs chosen by the priests made their way to Orongo for the birdman competition. Some competed directly, but most chose a *hopu manu,* or champion, to act on their behalf. After ritual preparations, the *hopu manu* descended the thousand-foot-high cliff face and swam a half mile to Motu Nui, where they camped and searched until one of them found a tern egg. After signaling his success to those assembled above by calling out and holding the egg aloft, the victorious *hopu manu* swam back and ascended the cliffs to Orongo. There he presented the egg to the chief for whom he competed, who assumed the position of birdman for the ensuing year.

As with the *moai* religion, the art of the birdman rites found its greatest expression in stone carving. Artists carved hundreds of birdman images—

25. Métraux 1940, pp. 311–15.
26. Van Tilburg 1994, p. 133.
27. This description of the birdman rites is based primarily on Van Tilburg 1994, pp. 58–60.

Figure 4. View from the cliffs at Orongo. The islet farthest offshore is Motu Nui, where champions chosen by the island's chiefs sought the first sooty tern egg during the annual rites of the birdman religion.

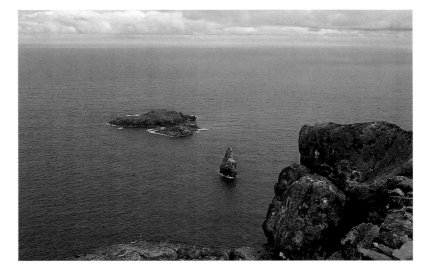

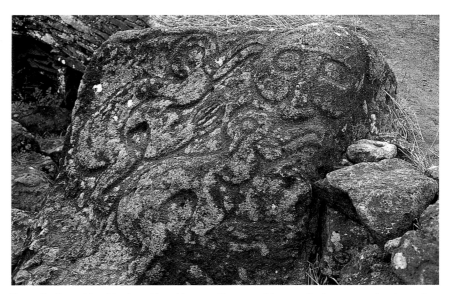

Figure 5. Carved boulder from Mata Ngara at Orongo, with petroglyphs representing the god Makemake as a crouching birdman. The skull-like face may also be a Makemake image.

28. Routledge 1919, p. 263.
29. Métraux 1940, p. 313; Van Tilburg 1994, pp. 57–58.
30. Geiseler 1883, pp. 31–33; Van Tilburg 1994, pl. 19.
31. Métraux 1940, p. 316.

which take the form of human figures with the heads and tails of birds—directly into the rock at Orongo. Ranging from shallow incised outlines to figures in high relief, birdman images cover virtually the entire surface of the dramatic basalt outcrop known as Mata Ngara (fig. 5). The images represent Makemake but also may record the individual birdmen who served as his earthly representatives.[28] In addition, a number of skull-like faces, possibly representing another form of Makemake, are present, as well as hundreds of stylized vulvas (*komari*) perhaps connected with adolescent initiation ceremonies that were held at the site.[29] One ceremonial structure at Orongo also housed a small *moai* known as Hoa Hakananai'a, whose back was adorned with birdmen, *komari,* dance paddles, and other images connected with the birdman religion.

In addition to rock art, a number of other works were associated with the birdman rites, including painted dance paddles and a unique series of wall paintings inside the ceremonial houses at Orongo depicting dance paddles, birds, European ships, and other motifs. The island's rare wood birdman figures might have been used during feasts associated with the birdman ceremonies. A unique barkcloth effigy that appears to be a ritual headdress (see cat. no. 38)—possibly representing Makemake in skull-like form—also might have played a part in the birdman rites.[30]

While the powers of Makemake and other *atua* extended throughout the island, the spirits (*akuaku*) generally were associated with particular families or with locations where they were believed to reside. Spirits could manifest themselves in human or animal form as well as in natural phenomena, such as landslides or heavy rain. In human guise, they could assume characteristics of either sex and, in some instances, marry and have children with ordinary people. Some *akuaku* were believed to be spirits of the dead and might have been venerated as family ancestors. Others were said to take the form of fantastic supernatural creatures.[31]

Many of Easter Island's *moai miro,* or wood images, likely represent *akuaku.* In some oral traditions, the skeletal images known as *moai kavakava* (see cat. nos. 7–10) and the flat female figures called *moai papa* (see cat. nos. 11, 12) are said to be likenesses of *akuaku* seen by the carver Tuu-ko-ihu, one of the original settlers.[32] The names attributed to the various types of *moai miro—moai kavakava* (image with ribs), *moai tangata* (image of a man), *moai papa* (flat image), *moko* (lizard), and *tangata manu* (birdman)— are all essentially descriptive and may represent classifications developed by the Rapa Nui in the late nineteenth century. Many of Easter Island's barkcloth images (*manu uru*)[33] are similar in form and iconography to some types of wood figures. These images possibly represent *akuaku*; however, they may also be miniature versions of *paina*, larger barkcloth effigies used in rituals honoring deceased parents and described in several early historic accounts.

As is the case with many of Easter Island's art forms, the precise significance of the barkcloth images will likely remain uncertain. This uncertainty, however, stems not from any mystery as to the origins of the art, but from the island's tragic postcontact history. When European explorers ended Easter Island's long isolation, they encountered its religious and artistic traditions intact. Although the trees used to transport them had been depleted long before, the *moai* still stood, and their creators and subject matter were still well known through oral tradition. The birdman rituals flourished, and artists continued to fashion images of the island's diverse *atua* and *akuaku* as well as ornaments to adorn prominent men and women. Much of this unique artistic heritage, the achievement of a millennium of solitude, would soon vanish or be radically transformed as a result of European contact.

The first encounters between Rapa Nui and Europeans were fleeting. After the Dutch rediscovered the island in 1722, it was next visited in 1770 by a Spanish expedition under Don Felipe González de Haedo, followed by Cook in 1774 and the French explorer La Pérouse in 1786. These first brief, occasionally violent, contacts almost certainly had a profound psychological impact on the Rapa Nui, even though all of the eighteenth-century expeditions combined spent less than a month ashore. Beginning in the nineteenth century, however, contacts became increasingly frequent. Explorers continued to touch at the island, but there were also more violent encounters with whalers and, as early as 1804, with slave ships seeking to supply the growing demand for labor in Peruvian guano mines and plantations.

Ironically, while the early nineteenth century witnessed increasing social disruption on Easter Island, it was also during this period that the island's wood sculpture enjoyed its greatest efflorescence. Wood images likely existed from the time of first settlement, but most of the finest examples date to the first half of the nineteenth century, when a greater technical virtuosity in carving was made possible through the introduction of steel tools and in some instances by supplies of imported wood. Both helped the island's master carvers to fashion some of the supreme expressions of Easter Island's distinctive religious imagery.

This brief burst of artistic activity was severely curtailed beginning in 1862, however, when twenty-two slave ships raided Easter Island in rapid

32. Routledge 1919, p. 270; Métraux 1940, pp. 260–61.
33. Métraux 1940, p. 265.

34. McCall 1976, pp. 296–306; Van Tilburg 1992, p. 25.

35. Métraux 1940, p. 43.

36. Numbering in the thousands at first contact, by 1868 Easter Island's population had declined to about nine hundred and reached its lowest ebb in 1872 at 111. Van Tilburg 1992, p. 28; Métraux 1940, p. 3. Today roughly four thousand people live on the island, about half of whom have at least some Rapa Nui ancestry. Paul Trachtman, conversation with the author, 2001.

37. Van Tilburg 1992, p. 27.

38. See Routledge 1919.

39. See Métraux 1940.

40. Varnedoe 1984, pp. 188–90, 195–97.

41. Ibid., pp. 191–92.

succession.[34] In total, an estimated eight hundred to a thousand islanders, including the *ariki mau* and nearly all of the high chiefs and priests, were abducted and put to work, primarily in guano mines on islands off the coast of Peru. When the Peruvian government ordered their repatriation the following year, only about a hundred survived, eighty-five of whom died before reaching home.[35] The dozen or so survivors brought smallpox to the island, further decimating the population.[36] Into this atmosphere of death and uncertainty arrived the first Catholic missionary, Eugène Eyraud, in 1864. Forced by the Rapa Nui to leave soon afterward, he later returned with a larger missionary party in 1866, and by 1868 the entire population reportedly had been baptized.[37]

As a result of the tragic events of the 1860s, much of Easter Island's original artistic and cultural heritage was lost. What information remains was for the most part recorded decades later. Throughout the latter half of the nineteenth century, scientific expeditions continued to visit the island, and many of them assembled substantial collections of its art. Among the more significant were the British on H.M.S. *Topaze* in 1868, the French on *La Flore* in 1872, and the Americans on U.S.S. *Mohican* in 1886. All three expeditions collected wood figures and ornaments as well as stone *moai*. In 1888, nine Rapa Nui chiefs signed a treaty ceding Easter Island to the Chilean government, and the island today is part of Chile.

The first systematic attempt to document surviving knowledge of Rapa Nui art and culture did not occur until 1914, when the pioneering ethnologist Katherine Routledge and her husband spent a year on the island recording its oral traditions and excavating several archaeological sites.[38] They were followed in 1934 by the Franco-Belgian Expedition, whose ethnographer, Alfred Métraux, combined his original research with published sources to produce what remains the most comprehensive account of Rapa Nui culture.[39]

As early as the 1870s, however, recognition of the accomplishments of Easter Island's master carvers had begun to extend beyond scientific circles. In the late nineteenth and early twentieth centuries, a broader appreciation for African, Oceanic, and other indigenous art forms began to flower among European artists and intellectuals. Julien Viaud, a young sailor aboard *La Flore* when it touched at the island in 1872, later achieved fame as a writer and artist under the pseudonym Pierre Loti. His largely fanciful depictions of the island—as a dreamlike world whose inhabitants live languidly, if somewhat furtively, amid the ruins of a heroic past—reflect the romanticized conceptions of Polynesian peoples that prevailed in the late nineteenth century (fig. 6).

Wood objects from Easter Island were among the diverse Oceanic art traditions to influence the works of Paul Gauguin. His sculpture *Wood Cylinder with Christ on the Cross* (1891–92; private collection) incorporates an image closely related to the *moai tangata*, and his 1893 canvas *Merahi metua no Tehamana (Te Hamana Has Many Parents)* (Art Institute of Chicago) shows the artist's Polynesian lover seated before a beam embellished with enlarged characters from the *rongorongo* tablets.[40] It is unclear whether Gauguin, who never visited the island, saw actual examples of Easter Island sculpture or worked from published photographs.[41]

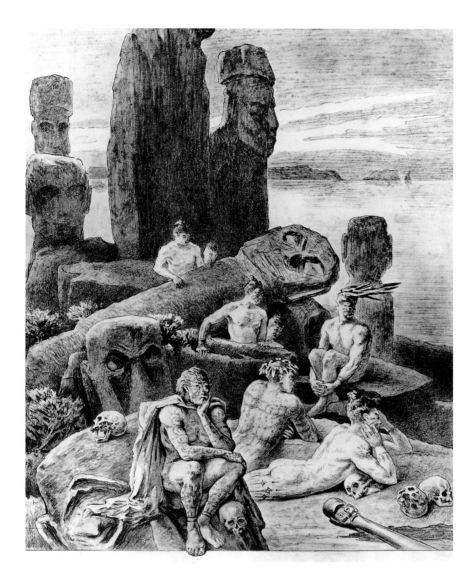

Figure 6. Pierre Loti (1850–1923). *L'Île de Pâques, 7 Janvier 1872, vers 5 heures du matin,* 1872. Watercolor, 7³⁄₄ x 11 in. (19.7 x 27.9 cm). Stéphen-Chauvet 1935, pl. 9, fig. 15

In the early twentieth century, Easter Island objects were collected by European artists and writers as well as by a growing number of art collectors as part of the enthusiasm for what was then known as "primitive" art. One of the first to champion the appreciation of Rapa Nui objects as works of art was the Latvian-born artist Voldemar Matvejs (1877–1914), a member of the Russian avant-garde. In 1914 Matvejs published *The Art of Easter Island,* the earliest known book to approach Rapa Nui works from an aesthetic perspective.[42]

Objects from Easter Island and other regions of Oceania later became important sources of inspiration for the Surrealists. In the fanciful "Surrealist Map of the World," published in 1929, the archipelagoes of the Pacific occupy a central position and are greatly enlarged, reflecting the import the movement accorded Oceanic art.[43] Within this already surreal geography Easter Island looms even larger, expanded to nearly the size of South America. A number of prominent Surrealists, including André Breton and Wolfgang

42. Bužinska 2000, pp. 89–93.
43. Maurer 1984, pp. 555–56.

21

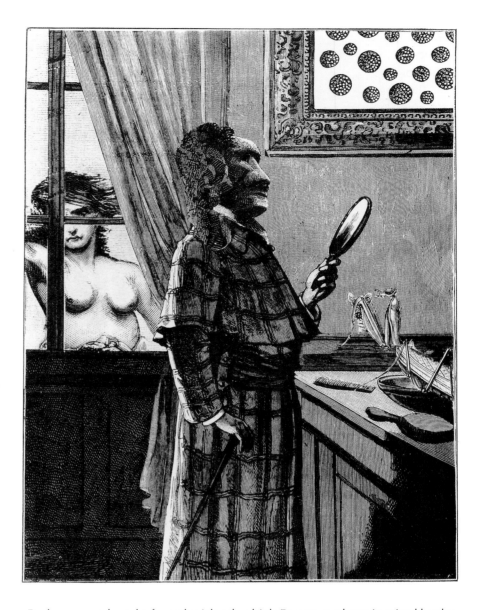

44. Peltier 1984, p. 113.
45. Maurer 1984, p. 551.
46. Ibid., pp. 553–59.

Paalen, owned works from the island, which Breton, perhaps inspired by the ruined *moai,* called the "modern Athens of Oceania."[44] Other Surrealists, such as André Masson, created paintings whose imagery was directly inspired by *moai* and other Rapa Nui art forms.[45]

Perhaps no Western artist was more profoundly influenced by Easter Island imagery than Max Ernst. In both his life and his work, Ernst assumed various artistic personas. One of these was "Loplop," a mythical avian being based in part on the Easter Island birdman. A number of Ernst's paintings also include birdman images inspired directly by the rock carvings at Orongo. In his 1934 collage novel *Une Semaine de Bonté,* the illustrations include bird-headed humans as well as a series of nine collages, collectively titled *L'Île de Pâques* (Easter Island), depicting humans with the heads of *moai* (fig. 7).[46]

The 1930s saw a growing appreciation of Easter Island art by European art collectors, among them the Parisian Charles Stéphen-Chauvet. In 1935 he published the lavishly illustrated volume *L'Île de Pâques et ses mystères,* devoted largely to the island's art. Although the works included are of varying aesthetic quality, the book was, and remains, influential in defining the canon of Easter Island art in the West.[47]

The artistic and intellectual climate that fostered this new appreciation of Easter Island art largely disappeared with the outbreak of World War II, and in the decades that followed the island's wood sculptures were mostly forgotten. The *moai*, however, achieved great notoriety with the publication in 1958 of Thor Heyerdahl's popular book *Aku Aku,* describing his expedition to the island. In contemporary popular culture, *moai* have become icons of the exotic, appearing in countless books and films as well as in more outlandish incarnations at souvenir shops and novelty restaurants.

On the island itself, Rapa Nui culture has in recent years enjoyed a renaissance. The arts of wood and stone carving, which never died out, are being reinvigorated, as are Polynesian music and dance. Many *moai* have been reerected by modern archaeologists and once again keep watch over the descendants of their original creators. The aesthetic richness of the island's other artistic traditions, so admired by the early modernists, is today being rediscovered by a new generation of artists and scholars. The enduring appeal of these works is a testament to the remarkable achievements of Rapa Nui artists—the legacy of a long, at times troubled, but ultimately splendid isolation.

47. Catalogue numbers 1, 4, 6, 7, 16, 39–42, 48, and 50 are among the works that appear in Stéphen-Chauvet's book.

Changing Faces: Rapa Nui Statues in the Social Landscape

Jo Anne Van Tilburg

1. For the current count, see Van Tilburg and Vargas Casanova 1998, p. 190; see also Thomson 1891; Routledge 1919; Englert 1948; Skjølsvold 1961; Cristino Ferrando, Vargas Casanova, and Izaurieta San Juan 1981; Van Tilburg 1986a, 1994.
2. The highest-ranked priests (*ivi atua*) were also Miru, and their gods included Tiki, the traditional Polynesian first man and creator. On Mangareva, Miru and his brother, Moa, are the traditional first settlers who arrived from Hiva, an undetermined or mythical homeland. In Polynesian myth, the Miru were associated with the western portion of the underworld. Buck 1938, pp. 20, 471. On Mangareva, a drum called *miru* was beaten continuously to accompany a chant (*ivitua*) performed by *rongorongo* experts during *marae* ceremonies honoring pregnancies and births in chiefly families. Ibid., p. 104. These are provocative parallels between Mangarevan and Rapa Nui culture. Moreover, on Mangaia in the Cook Islands, as on Rapa Nui, only one "tribe" was entitled to the title *ariki*. Métraux 1940, p. 129.

Easter Island—or Rapa Nui, as the island and its people are now known—is not at first glance a place one would expect to find an impressive megalithic tradition. Nonetheless, the Polynesian settlers who arrived in the second half of the first millennium A.D. carved some 887 magnificent stone statues (*moai* or, less commonly, *moai maea*).[1] This impressive feat was, in part, an adaptive social process in which the deeply rooted traditions and cultural values held by the original settlers were tempered through interaction with the island's landscape and environment. Modern archaeology has precisely described the *moai*—their form, style, placement, distribution, and relationships within Rapa Nui's built environment and settlement pattern—but very few hints exist as to how the statues functioned in precontact society. Geography and archaeology represent history on the ground; if we examine that history in the context of Rapa Nui aesthetics, ethnography, and ecology, we can infer aspects of how the *moai* might have been used. A broader context is also provided by comparing the social structures and developmental patterns of Rapa Nui culture with other discrete but historically related Polynesian chiefdoms.

The quarry for 95 percent of all known *moai* was the volcanic crater Rano Raraku on the island's eastern end. The crater is composed of consolidated lapilli tuff (compressed volcanic ash), a visually distinctive material that the Rapa Nui used only for *moai*. When freshly cut, the tuff is yellow-red, a highly prized, sacred color that was similar to Rapa Nui body paints made from red mineralized tuff (*kiea*), which they pulverized in a stone mortar, or from turmeric (*pua* or *renga*), made by grating the tumeric plant into stone basins called *taheta*. Rano Raraku tuff is relatively easy to carve and, despite randomly interspersed nodules of dark, dense metamorphic rock, it can take a smooth polish. Although it varies in density (thus statues of the same size can vary in weight), weathers rapidly, and is naturally friable, the tuff nevertheless proved to be a near-perfect sculptural material for the Rapa Nui. When carved into *moai,* it symbolically represented the chiefly body adorned in sacred red.

Rapa Nui society was a hereditary chiefdom until the death of the last recognized paramount chief in 1866. The ruling elite were regarded as equals of the gods. The island was subdivided into communal parcels of land (*kainga*) held by ten major lineages (*mata*). Each parcel had a primary ceremonial structure (*ahu*) that proclaimed the identity of the landholders. Functionally similar to other Polynesian temples and ceremonial grounds (*marae*), Rapa Nui *ahu* were built of locally quarried volcanic stone that varied in quality. The designs and placement of *ahu* were dictated by available resources but fit within a well-established, island-wide architectural pattern. Differing degrees of stoneworking skill are evident in the construction of *ahu*; some seaward walls, such as those of Ahu Tahiri, at Vinapu, show great stonecutting expertise and time-consuming attention to joinery, while others, perhaps built by lineages with fewer resources or a less cohesive organization, are more roughly finished.

Small *ahu* were probably established shortly after first settlement, thought to have been about A.D. 800. Over time, they were elaborated to support bigger, heavier, and more numerous statues. The largest, most complex *ahu* were built along the coastline, and each lineage had resource-use rights that extended seaward from the *ahu* as well as inland, toward their gardens and plantations.

Beginning about 1000 to 1100 at the latest, *moai* carved at Rano Raraku began to be raised on coastal *ahu* and situated to face inland, overlooking the houses of the elite. The status of a household decreased in proportion to its distance from the *ahu*. The different lineages, which over time grew, prospered, and segmented, later consolidated into two island-wide political alliances that were probably the result of long-established hereditary status divisions.

The western alliance, Ko Tu'u, was the higher ranking of the two districts, and its most prestigious site was Anakena, home of the aristocratic Miru lineage and of the paramount chief (*ariki mau*).[2] Considered a divine being, the *ariki mau* descended from the gods Tangaroa and Rongo through Hotu Matu'a, or "great parent," by tradition the island's founding ancestor.[3] Potent spiritual power (*mana*) capable of increasing the fertility of the natural world was concentrated in the *ariki mau*'s sacred head, loins, and hands, and his person was considered *tapu,* or set apart, both physically and spiritually. It seems no coincidence, then, that all *moai* have exquisitely detailed facial features and hands, and that some oral traditions suggest the statues were phallic symbols.

The more populous but lower-ranking eastern district, Hotu Iti, included Rano Raraku—a fortuitous and presumably prestigious accident of geography—as well as Ahu Tongariki, the largest *ahu* on the island.[4] By about 1500, Ahu Tongariki had been rebuilt, expanded, and elaborated at least three times and was surmounted by fifteen large and very heavy *moai* weighing up to about 88 metric tons (194,000 pounds) each. The lineages of the eastern district that accomplished this feat lacked the long history of internal cohesion that distinguished the higher-ranked Miru lineage in the west. Ahu Tongariki not only represented the eastern district's highest level of internal political integration, it also established Hotu Iti as a major political challenger to traditional Miru authority. By 1500 both districts could lay claim to the tallest *moai* on an *ahu*—in the west, one was successfully raised at Te Pito Kura that measured approximately 9.8 meters in height (fig. 8); in the east, a *moai* destined for Hanga Te Tenga stood 9.94 meters tall but fell as it was being erected.

In addition to Rano Raraku tuff, other rare or unique natural materials on Rapa Nui had symbolic value. For example, Rapa Nui has no coral reefs,

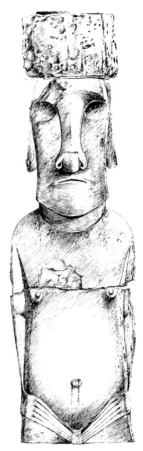

Figure 8. Conjectural reconstruction of Moai Paro at Ahu Te Pito Kura, the tallest *moai* erected on an *ahu* and the last one left standing. It was thrown down and broken between 1834 and 1864. H. 9.8 m (32 ft. 2 in.). Drawing by Cristián Arévalo Pakarati, 1998

3. Links have been suggested between Hotu Matu'a and 'Atu Motua, or "one of the same name," in Mangareva. Green 1998, p. 109; see also Buck 1938; Emory 1939.
4. Cristino Ferrando and Vargas Casanova 1998.

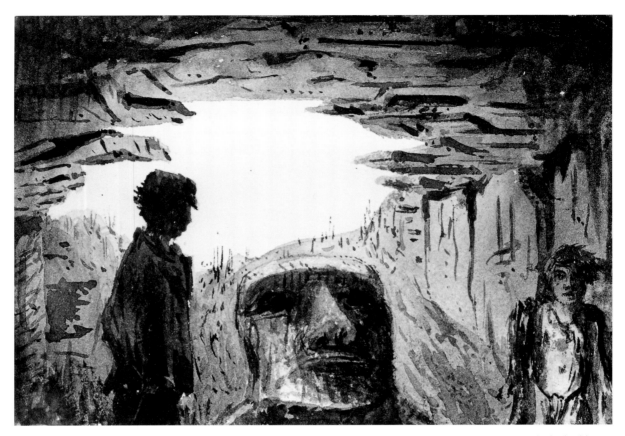

Figure 9. Sketch by Lt. Matthew James Harrison, H.M.S. *Topaze*, depicting the *moai* Hoa Hakananai'a in situ inside the building at Orongo called "Taura-renga," 1868. British Museum, London

5. Van Tilburg 1986b.

and although the scarcity of coral might have fluctuated over time, it was never common and was used selectively. Small chunks of coral served as abraders (*punga*) to smooth the surfaces of *moai*. Larger pieces were carved into superbly crafted eyes for the *moai,* the pupils of which were made of red scoria, a type of volcanic rock. Both red scoria and coral were scattered over burials or crematoria. Red scoria was also used as fascia or corner-stones in *ahu*, carved into the distinctive cylindrical headdresses (*pukao*) that sat atop about one hundred *moai,* and sculpted into ceremonial basins and both megalithic and portable figures.[5]

It is highly unlikely that each of the more than three hundred *moai* that once stood upright on *ahu* had its own set of coral-and-red scoria eyes, or that the eyes were always in place. A limited number were probably kept by the high priests and inserted only during important ceremonies attended by the *ariki mau*. Once set into the *moai,* the eyes activated the ancestral spirit within. The presence of the *ariki mau* was thereby made graphically visible and proclaimed to all, while his dangerous *mana* was contained, focused, or controlled.

Rano Kau, a majestic volcano that rises 324 meters (1,063 feet) above sea level, anchors the extreme southwest tip of Rapa Nui. From the time of first settlement Rano Kau was a significant feature in the island's sacred traditions, and it later included the site of Orongo, a ceremonial "village" devoted to the cult of the creator god Makemake. The crater of Rano Kau, long kept secret from outsiders, was first described by French explorers in 1786. The ceremonies at Orongo continued until 1866, when the last paramount chief died. Although at least three foreign expeditions had visited Orongo by 1900, the site was not investigated systematically until the arrival of Katherine and William Scoresby Routledge, coleaders of the Mana Expedition to Easter Island (1913–15).

Orongo had blossomed into an island-wide ceremonial center by about 1500. The major components of the site were a small *ahu,* a concentration of petroglyphs emblematic of the birdman (*tangata manu*) ideology and aesthetic tradition, and buildings made of stone slabs, which were divided, like the island and the crater, into Ko Tu'u and Hotu Iti ownership.[6] Offshore of Orongo lay important satellite sites on three tiny islets, the most important of which was Motu Nui, a seasonal seabird rookery (see fig. 4). Orongo ritual focused on birds, birds' eggs, and fish, and the deity at its center was Makemake, who had taken on the characteristics of the earlier Miru god Tiki.

In 1868, H.M.S. *Topaze,* an English frigate on an extensive cruise through the Marquesas and Society Islands, called at Rapa Nui to verify its position on admiralty charts and to conduct a brief survey. Two *Topaze* crew members found an unusual basalt *moai* in a building at Orongo called Taura-renga. According to Richard Sainthill, secretary to *Topaze* captain Richard A. Powell, this *moai,* known as Hoa Hakananai'a, was "buried to its shoulders in the ground opposite one of the doors." A sketch of Hoa Hakananai'a in situ was made by Lieutenant Matthew J. Harrison (fig. 9).[7] The building that housed it belonged to the Miru, and the statue faced toward their lands. Stylistically Hoa Hakananai'a is fully within the *moai* tradition—the statue's proportions and features are the same as those of other *moai.* It is also embellished with a dorsal "ring-and-girdle" design that probably represents a belt and loincloth (*hami*), a distinctive feature of the *moai* first described by Katherine Routledge. Variants of this design also occur on both tuff and red scoria *moai.*[8] In historical times, Hoa Hakananai'a was adorned with red and white paint or red-stained barkcloth during rites of passage and initiation. Superimposed on its midback, shoulders, head, and ears are well-carved birdmen (*tangata manu*), ceremonial dance paddles (*rapa*), birds (*manu*), and vulva forms (*komari*). These designs are all emblematic of elements of Orongo rituals. Their presence on Hoa Hakananai'a, as well as the statue's placement—in a Miru building facing Miru land—link this *moai,* and the Orongo traditions, to the Miru.

Sainthill recorded that on the morning following its discovery, Hoa Hakananai'a "left the house in which he had so long dwelt, and two days after was floated off to the ship, amidst the cheers of the islanders."[9] In December 1886, an American ship, U.S.S. *Mohican,* called at Rapa Nui. Paymaster William J. Thomson and others conducted a brief but valuable survey and asked to be shown a *moai* similar to Hoa Hakananai'a. They were taken to Ahu O'Pepe, where they found a *moai* that, like Hoa Hakananai'a, was carved of basalt (fig. 10).[10] This statue was placed on a wood sled and dragged about two-and-a-half miles before being loaded aboard the *Mohican,* ultimately destined for the Smithsonian Institution's National Museum of Natural History, Washington, D.C., where it remains today.

6. Routledge 1920; Ferdon 1961. Rapa Nui always used the word *ana,* or cave, when discussing the Orongo buildings, never *hare,* or house. Routledge n.d. *Hare,* used throughout late ethnographic and other Rapa Nui literature, is a complete misnomer in light of the documented use of the structures. Three Rapa Nui men provided information on the ownership of the "houses" to Katherine Routledge, and she carefully cross-checked her data for reliability.

7. Van Tilburg 1992, p. 40. Harrison's sketch is one of four known drawings that he made while on Rapa Nui. They were located in 1997 by Dorota Starzecka, then assistant keeper at the British Museum, with the assistance of K. Chettleburgh, Harrison's granddaughter, as part of our continuing research into the subject of H.M.S. *Topaze* on Rapa Nui. Ibid., p. 95, n. 18; see also Routledge n.d.

8. Routledge 1919, 1920; Van Tilburg 1987, 1988, 1994.

9. Van Tilburg 1992, p. 40.

10. Routledge 1919, figs. 31, 106; Thomson 1891, pl. 28; Cooke 1899, p. 700. Variant spellings of Ahu O'Pepe are: "Ahu A Pépe" (two stones marking the boundary between Tongariki and Hangaroa) (Routledge n.d., p. 131); Ahu-a-pepe (Métraux 1940, p. 349); Ahu A'Pepe (Barthel 1978, p. 259); and Ahu O-Pepe (Campbell 1987, p. 145). A Rapa Nui family of the Tupahotu Rikiriki lineage (*mata*) claims the site today and calls it Ahu O'Pepe. According to Alberto Hotus, it might have been named after Ko Pepe, the man "who commissioned the *ahu.*" Ko Pepe was the son of Ko Heki'i, for whom a large coastal *ahu* is named. María Aifiti Engepito Ika Tetono, wife of the renowned Rapa Nui informant Juan Tepano, a Tupahotu, was Miru descended from this line. Hotus et al. 1988, p. 219.

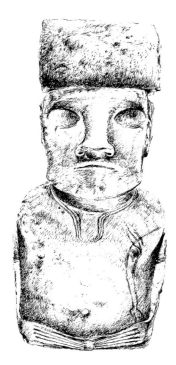
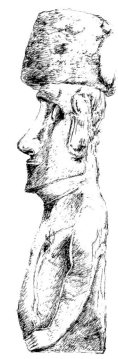

Figure 10. Two views of the *moai* and *pukao* collected by U.S.S. *Mohican*, 1886. H. of complete figure: 2.24 m (7 ft. 4 in.). Drawing by Cristián Arévalo Pakarati, 2000

A head of Rano Raraku tuff (cat. no. 1) was collected at the same time (see fig. 11).[11] Its features, like those of all *moai,* are well formed, balanced, harmonious, and framed on both sides by curved facial planes. The elongated jaw is emphasized, and the artificially extended earlobes are detailed in finely incised lines. The delicately carved nostrils are rendered as bas-relief fishhook shapes, and the mouth is narrow, with slightly upraised lips, which, although compressed, are clearly separated. The eye sockets are oval, their outer edges flush with the side plane of the face. The backs of the sockets have a slight ridge along the bottom to allow for the insertion of the coral-and-red scoria eyes, which would have looked slightly upward. Intact, the original *moai* would have been slightly under 2.5 meters tall as it stood on Ahu O'Pepe, gazing out over the homes and gardens of the Tupahotu Rikiriki lineage.

The *Mohican* also collected a red scoria *pukao*—or "topknot," which originally sat atop the head of a *moai*—although it may not have come from Ahu O'Pepe. Thought to represent red feather crowns, barkcloth headdresses, or red-stained hair, *pukao* usually were present only on *moai* at much larger, coastal sites.

PRODUCTION, TRANSPORT, AND DISTRIBUTION

The tools and methods of *moai* production relate closely to other Polynesian technologies, particularly canoe construction and house building. Experts who performed such sacred work were organized into powerful "guilds," each with its own insignia, gods, and priests. A team of *moai* carvers (*tangata maori anga moai maea*) worked under a master carver (*tangata honui maori*).[12] Statues were commissioned by lineage heads and the carvers paid with costly foods such as lobster, eel, and tuna. *Moai* carving was centered in the eastern district; however, legends say it originated in the west among the ancestral Miru.

There were five stages in *moai* production. First, a blank, roughly rectangular block of stone was quarried—and, sometimes, partially undercut—and held in place with smaller stones. Varying numbers of carvers, as many as fifteen at a time on larger statues, performed this work using basalt picks (*toki*). The master carver and an assistant or apprentice then added the fine details in a predetermined sequence, usually beginning with the head and face. A central line running from nose to navel was laid down by the master carver, which facilitated the desired bilateral symmetry in the torso, arms, and hands. Specialists then finished any necessary undercutting and a larger workforce used ropes and levers to move the *moai* down the slope of the quarry. It was then set upright in an excavated pit. Here all the details save the carved eye sockets were finished and the surface polished with coral abraders.

11. An incomplete survey and sketch map is given in Campbell 1987, p. 145. A corrected survey and map are in Van Tilburg and Vargas Casanova 1988; Van Tilburg 1992; Van Tilburg 1994, p. 134. With the removal of the head by the *Mohican*, there are now seven torsos at Ahu O'Pepe but only six heads. There is no evidence that *pukao* were present, but at least one—the specimen collected by *Mohican*—might have been. See also Routledge 1919, p. 234.
12. Métraux 1940, p. 137.

The methods of transporting *moai* likely varied and were adapted to accommodate the size of the statue, available natural resources and food, and the terrain. Experimental archaeology has shown that forty Rapa Nui men and women can efficiently pull a statistically average *moai*—about 4 meters tall and weighing 8 to 10 metric tons (17,500 to 22,000 pounds), depending on stone density—horizontally on an A-frame sled.[13] About three to four hundred more people, however, would have been necessary to produce the food, cordage, and other materials required to move and erect such a *moai*. Examples of larger moai, from 5 to 12 meters tall, still lie along roads leading from Rano Raraku. Although traditions name some of their intended destinations, there are no *ahu* prepared to receive them. Katherine Routledge suggested that these seemingly abandoned *moai* had stood upright in place, forming a ceremonial avenue connecting Rano Raraku and Rano Kau, but further research is needed to test this theory.

No matter what method was used to transport the *moai,* the intercession of priests was critical to ensure success. Three variations on a single Rapa Nui tradition, collected from the mid-1800s to 1914, offer the metaphorical view that *moai* "walked about in the darkness," "walked for a distance and then stopped," or were moved by "supernatural power."[14] Early explorers had seen, and Katherine Routledge heard, reliable accounts by Rapa Nui of tall, barkcloth-covered wood effigies raised in front of *ahu* and manipulated with attached ropes during ceremonial feasts honoring deceased parents (*paina*).[15] It is possible, then, that the traditions of "walking" *moai* are reliable but refer to these *paina* figures rather than to the megalithic sculptures.

13. Van Tilburg and Ralston 1999.
14. Thomson 1891, p. 497; Routledge 1919, p. 182; Métraux 1940, p. 304; Heyerdahl, Skjølsvold, and Pavel 1989, p. 36.
15. In 1770 the Spanish raised three crosses on the island with attendant pomp and ceremony, and the Rapa Nui, in turn, raised a 3.4-meter-tall wood-and-barkcloth human effigy that the Spanish thought was called Copeca and dedicated to (sexual) enjoyment. Métraux, however, says that *kopeka*, or *ati kopeka*, "always refers to a slain man and implies the idea of vengeance." Métraux 1940, p. 345. See also Churchill 1912, p. 306. On Mangareva, *kopeka* means "crossed" and refers to how two sprits are crossed at the deck of a raft to form a triangular sail. Buck 1938, p. 283. This suggests that the Rapa Nui term referred to the actual forms of the Spaniards' crosses—and to the effigy as the metaphorical "mast" (that is, the chief) around which Rapa Nui society organized itself—or to these uprights collectively as objects with similar physical characteristics.

Figure 11. *Moai* head (cat. no. 1) in situ at Ahu O'Pepe, 1886.

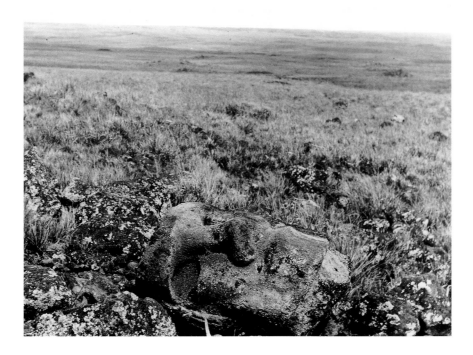

16. Cristino Ferrando and Vargas Casanova 1998; Martinsson-Wallin and Wallin 1998, p. 182.

17. "Living memory" was a common Victorian expression used often by Routledge (1919, p. 213). She learned from Viriamo—Juan Tepano's mother—and others about a *koro* ceremony at an *ahu* that very well could have been Ahu O'Pepe. Ibid., p. 234. Métraux also connects "Ahu-a-pepe" with a *koro*—he says it was attended by Tuu-ko-ihu, the legendary carver, and alludes to cannibalism. Métraux 1940, p. 349. In another tale Métraux collected (1940, p. 381) called "Pepe and His Wife," "Pepe" was a Miru cannibal whose wife denounced him to his enemies. Warriors "knocked the woman down with their clubs, she fell on her back and her vulva was seen." These stories may refer to, or account for, the superb bas-relief *komari* carving at the site.

18. Skjølsvold found burials and other post-*ahu* ritual activity associated with this *moai* (see fig. 12) in Rano Raraku. Skjølsvold 1961, pp. 354–55. Routledge originally excavated this statue between 1914 and 1915. Routledge n.d., p. 4. See also Van Tilburg and Lee 1987.

CLASSIFICATION AND DATING

All *moai* fall into one of four categories, or types, based on body and head shape: rounded, square (uncommon), rectangular (the most common), and trapezoidal. Although none can be dated directly by scientific methods currently available, statue types can be linked to specific phases of *ahu* construction and thus associated with radiocarbon dates for those phases. According to present evidence, the *ahu moai* phase of Rapa Nui prehistory began by 1000 to 1100. The earliest evidence of the presence of monolithic statues on *ahu* is at Ahu Nau Nau at Anakena, the traditional home of Hotu Matu'a.[16] Early *moai* fragments there dating prior to the fourteenth and fifteenth centuries exhibit similar stylistic characteristics—smaller, more rounded forms with proportionately sized ears, chins, and jaws. At Ahu Tongariki on the east coast, however, these rounded forms are replaced by rectangular and trapezoidal shapes, and the statues increase in size over time, culminating in the final *ahu* development phase with *moai* reaching from 5.6 to 8.7 meters tall. These later, bigger *moai* were being transported and erected during the same general time period when, on the other side of the island, Orongo had emerged as the central focus of the birdman religion.

The tall, slender *moai* so prominent on the interior and exterior slopes of Rano Raraku represent the last stage of the *moai* tradition, the apogee of its technology and artistry. As many as half were probably carved between 1500 and the mid-1600s, possibly slightly later. Most were not intended for placement on *ahu*. Instead, their positions in and around Rano Raraku emphasized the stone carving achievements, resource control, and claim to power of *moai* carvers as a class and of Hotu Iti as a district.

EMBELLISHMENT AND REUSE

Little is known of the original ceremonies held in connection with the *ahu moai*. One possible key to understanding the later reuse of the images lies in accounts of *ahu* ceremonies honoring deceased or living parents (*paina* and *koro*, respectively), some of which, as we have seen, included large barkcloth figures. Although no examples of *paina* figures survive, some small ones exist that may be functionally related. At Ahu O'Pepe, a *koro* ceremony took place within the "living memory" of some of Katherine Routledge's ethnographic informants.[17] She was told that a large crowd was feted with quantities of food and participants lavishly adorned with paint, tattoo, and wood ornaments. An older *moai* fragment at the site was expertly carved into a large, bas-relief *komari,* a symbol associated with female initiation rites at Orongo. Designs referring to body paint or tattoo were also superimposed on the clavicle of a *moai* torso as well as on the *moai* and *pukao* collected from this site by the *Mohican.* Similar motifs—as well as dots on the face, lines on the neck, *komari* on the top of the head, and numerous others—occur on other *moai* (fig. 12), the small barkcloth figures (see cat. nos. 24–26), and wood carvings.[18] This chronological layering of symbols reveals the strong continuity in Rapa Nui aesthetics from prehistoric to postcontact times and demonstrates the continuing importance of artisans, including stone and wood carvers and practitioners of tattoo, in ritual activities.

SPLENDID ISOLATION?

The defining characteristics of all *moai* include monumentality, skillful craftsmanship, formalism with little surface elaboration, an emphasis on facial features and hands, and innovation within a strictly defined canon of expressive modes. From the first roughing-out stages to their final, upright placement, *moai* represented a primal metaphor of creation enacted before the entire Rapa Nui community. They also reflected many aspects of the social changes and transformation of religious traditions that took place on Rapa Nui from about 1500 to the first contact with Europeans in 1722. This period saw a gradual decrease in the importance of *ahu*-based *moai* as ritual foci that coincides with the emergence of the Orongo rituals. At the same time, the increasing use of Rano Raraku's slopes to display finished *moai* was partially the result of the increasing scarcity of the wood needed to move them, but it also might have been a reflection of Hotu Iti's challenge to the traditional, religiously sanctioned Miru leadership of Ko Tu'u. The people of Hotu Iti attempted to validate this usurpation by clustering *moai,* the premier symbol of traditional hierarchical power, at Rano Raraku in numbers far beyond those that could have been moved and raised on individual lineage *ahu* in Ko Tu'u. Statue carvers and other experts in production would have been key figures in the implementation of this challenge.

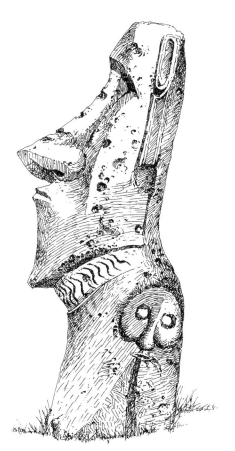

Figure 12. Profile view of a *moai* on the exterior slope of Rano Raraku, showing superimposed carved designs. H. 5.75 m (18 ft. 10³⁄₈ in.). Drawing by Cristián Arévalo Pakarati, 1995

Two models, supported by the contextual record of East Polynesia, can be suggested to account for these dramatic changes in Rapa Nui society. The first holds that after the initial Polynesian settlement, Rapa Nui culture evolved in isolation and subsequently crashed as a result of population pressure and the depletion of natural resources. The second model accepts this general scenario but also proposes that the arrival of a second group of Polynesian settlers by about 1500 may have accelerated nascent religious innovation and stimulated the florescence of the Orongo rituals. In both models, religion was a major mechanism for coping with or controlling social problems caused by environmental stress and for validating otherwise disruptive power shifts. At present, the archaeological record does not definitively support one hypothesis over the other, although that may change as East Polynesian interactive trade or resource networks are clarified through future research.[19]

The religious transformation of Rapa Nui culture was achieved in a context of increasingly intense environmental pressure and through interaction among those who structured belief (priests), those who objectified it (artisans), and those who manipulated it (chiefs). This transformation was no less remarkable than the megalithic tradition itself. *Moai,* in their various contexts and guises, were integral to all aspects of Rapa Nui religious and artistic traditions throughout the island's history. Their endurance is a testament to the genius of the *moai* as symbolic works and to their pivotal role in Rapa Nui culture.

19. Green 1998; Weisler 1998; Green and Weisler 2000. It should also be noted that at various times during Rapa Nui social development until about 1500, outward migration of some islanders and their cultural traditions was theoretically possible.

Rapa Nui Art and Aesthetics

Adrienne L. Kaeppler

1. As an adjective, *hakake* is defined as "active, agile, nimble, brave, cunning, or skillful"; as a noun, it means "ability, agility, courage, skillfulness, or talent." Fuentes 1960, p. 727.

2. Kaeppler 1989. By this definition, the arts occur in all known human societies. They are systems of knowledge—the products of action and interaction, as well as the processes through which action and interaction take place. These systems of knowledge are socially and culturally constructed—created by, known by, and agreed upon by a group of people and preserved primarily in memory. Although some art forms are ephemeral, they all have structured content, can be visual or aural manifestations of social relationships, may be the subjects of elaborate aesthetic systems, and often assist in the understanding of cultural values.

The art of Easter Island, or Rapa Nui, represents a distinct tradition within Polynesian art, but one with forms and concepts closely related to those elsewhere in Polynesia, especially the Marquesas Islands, Mangareva, Ra'ivavae (in the Cook Islands), Hawai'i, and Aotearoa (New Zealand). Rapa Nui, however, lies outside of the tropics, and it supports a physical environment, plants, and animals somewhat different from those found on most other Polynesian islands. Some plants—such as the paper mulberry tree used for making barkcloth, a traditional Polynesian textile—proved difficult to grow, and wood suitable for carving was in short supply. Colorful wild bird feathers were not available, so orange and black chicken feathers were substituted. These climatic differences, along with other limitations imposed by the available natural resources, helped to shape the aesthetics and social roles of Rapa Nui art.

In addition to stone carving and architecture—discussed by Jo Anne Van Tilburg in her essay in this volume—the arts of Rapa Nui included wood carving, fiber and textile arts, oratory, music, and movement-based forms. Through tattoo and body painting, the human body was also a medium for artistic and social expression, as it is throughout Polynesia. Rapa Nui wood carving, in particular, has been appreciated in the West. Since the mid-nineteenth century, museums and collectors have been acquiring examples of wood sculpture (*moai kavakava, moai papa, moai tangata, tangata manu,* and *moko*), long and short dance paddles (*'ao* and *rapa*), long and short staffs (*ua* and *paoa*), tablets with incised glyphs (*kohau rongorongo*), gorgets (*rei miro*), and carved egg- or coconut-shaped objects called *tahonga* (see frontispiece). The Rapa Nui often carved odd or curious pieces of wood into creative realistic forms, including animals such as lizards, sea eels, and birds.

But how should we use the word "art" in a Rapa Nui context, and how does Rapa Nui art express their societal values? To answer these questions, it helps to clarify our use of the term "art," as Polynesian languages have no words or concepts directly comparable with the Western meaning of the word. Polynesian languages do have, however, terms that deal with skillfulness, such as the Rapa Nui word *hakake*.[1] One can argue that Rapa Nui art can be conceived of as those cultural forms resulting from creative processes that use or manipulate—that is, handle with skill—words, sounds, movements, materials (including the human body), spaces, or scents in such a way as to formalize the nonformal. Aesthetics can consequently be defined as evaluative ways of thinking about these forms.[2]

Three basic concepts help us to understand Polynesian artistic traditions: skill, indirectness, and the intimate association of verbal and visual modes of expression. Terms dealing with skill in Polynesian languages often refer to any work, task, feat, trade, craft, or performance that requires specialized skill or ability. Indirectness was (and remains) highly developed and culturally valued—many Polynesian words have hidden or veiled meanings that must be unraveled layer by layer until the metaphors on which they are based become apparent. Objects cannot be understood simply through visual examination. Rather, they must be related to the social and cultural contexts in which they are used and evaluated according to Polynesian aesthetic principles. How an object was employed and its efficacy in ritual were often more important than how it looked.

The importance of an object was integrally linked with its owner's rank and status. There was a sensitivity to context—appropriate objects were to be used at appropriate times by appropriate people, depending on the reasons for the ritual and on who was present. Objects were chronicles of history made visible and inherited both as a physical form and as information. Persons, places, events, and emotions were commemorated and cherished through objects, which contributed to the objects' power (*mana*).

Rapa Nui artistic traditions were not primarily concerned with the external forms of objects. They took into account a range of other criteria: the process of fabricating the object from appropriate materials and using it within the limits of a specific context; the visual representation of status and rank within an ever-expanding symbolic system; the historical associations and sense of occasion manifest in an object and amplified by the passage of time; and the interrelationships among various artistic forms. In addition to an object's symbolism and history, its evolution over time—from its original form to any subsequent refurbishment or reuse—were all aspects of an aesthetic tradition that emphasized ongoing processes and changing uses.

RAPA NUI SCULPTURE IN HUMAN AND ANIMAL FORM

Figures in human form—whether of carved wood or barkcloth sewn over a base of reeds and other plant materials—probably represented ancestors. Wood figures proliferated during the nineteenth century, developing from eighteenth-century prototypes into several recognizable "classic" types. In the nineteenth-century literature on Rapa Nui, such figures were usually termed *moai miro,* or figures of wood. The classic male figures now known as *moai kavakava* are characterized by an emaciated appearance and often have bas-relief designs carved on the tops of their heads. Female figures (*moai papa*) have flat bodies and elegant hands carved in low relief. The more naturalistic *moai tangata* are male figures with filled-out, rounded bodies; *tangata manu* combine the features of men and birds; and *moko* combine features of men and lizards.

The most prominent characteristics of *moai kavakava* are their well-carved backbones and rib cages (see cat. nos. 7–10). The back, especially the backbone, is an important, recurring feature of Rapa Nui imagery. The spinal column is often well carved, with pronounced notches between the vertebrae. A circle, perhaps representing a belt, and a vertical strip, perhaps depicting a

3. Kaeppler 1982.
4. The Kū gods are a group of Hawaiian deities bearing distinct but related names, such as Kukailimoku or Kunuiakea.

loincloth (*hami*), are symbolic representations of clothing, but they occur only on the backs of the figures. The ribs of the wood figures appear to be primarily elaborations of the backbone that add to its overall three-dimensional quality. Similar backbones and rib cages are seen in the *tangata manu* and *moko* figures.

The conceptual framework of Rapa Nui sculpture can be compared with those of Aotearoa and Hawai'i. In each case, the backbone appears to be an important genealogical symbol. The notched Rapa Nui backbone is similar to the notched *whakapapa* (genealogical objects carved from wood or bone) of the Māori, in which the notches represent succeeding generations of ancestors. The three-dimensionality of the backbone and rib cages of Rapa Nui *moai kavakava* and *moko* can also be compared with the structure of Māori meetinghouses, whose ridgepoles are considered to be their backbones and their rafters the ribs of an encompassing ancestor.

A number of Hawaiian sculptures with well-defined spinal columns have been associated with genealogical concepts symbolically linked to Lono, the god of peace and agriculture.[3] In Hawai'i, figures of Lono became metaphors for the sacred and social importance of genealogy and of a family that works together in harmony, concepts manifest in agriculture and other peaceful pursuits. The Lono figures contrast with those of the Kū gods,[4] which can be considered as metaphors for larger social groups and emphasize competition and warfare.

Although we have little direct evidence of the meanings and uses of Rapa Nui figures, I suggest that Rapa Nui wood figures, like Hawaiian Lono figures, incorporated genealogical metaphors of social importance and were used in peaceful contexts that focused on family, agriculture, and fertility. These wood figures thus contrast with the stone *moai maea*, which, like the Kū figures in Hawai'i, were connected with issues of competition and warfare involving society as a whole and were invoked on important occasions affecting the larger social group. The relationship between the Rapa Nui wood and stone figures, then, was similar to the paired opposition of Lono and Kū in Hawai'i—opposites that nevertheless reflect aspects of one another.

Wood and stone images, respectively, may be said to be symbolic of the cooperative and competitive aspects of Rapa Nui life—or, put another way, as metaphors for the intimate association between two opposing social forces manifest as ancestors and gods. Wood figures, symbolic of cooperation within the extended family, were worn at feasts and other peaceful occasions related to family ancestors, whereas stone sculptures, symbolizing competing social groups, were invoked at rituals related to lineage ancestors or gods.

BARKCLOTH FIGURES AND THEIR WOOD COUNTERPARTS

In some parts of Polynesia, sculptures were made not only of wood but also of other materials, such as the feather-covered wickerwork images of Hawai'i. I suggest that among the Rapa Nui, barkcloth was a high-status substitute for wood. Wood for carving was rare, but barkcloth was rarer still

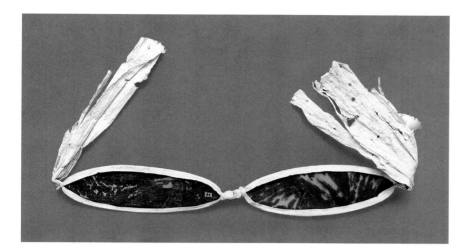

Figure 13. Belt. 19th century. Turtleshell and barkcloth, L. 144 cm (56¾ in.). British Museum, London

5. Forster 1986, p. 332.

and, perhaps, even more important. In the eighteenth and nineteenth centuries, the Rapa Nui were especially eager to obtain barkcloth when trading with ships that had called elsewhere in Polynesia. When Captain James Cook visited Rapa Nui in 1774 during his second Pacific voyage, Tahitian barkcloth was in great demand among the Rapa Nui. In exchange, they gave feather headdresses and other objects, including several wood images acquired by Mahine, a Tahitian man traveling with Cook as an interpreter.[5]

Where Hawaiian chiefs wore red feather cloaks to cover their backbones, which were symbolically associated with their sacred genealogies, Rapa Nui chiefs wore barkcloth cloaks. The highest-status individuals, such as the paramount chief (*ariki mau*) and his family, also covered the tops of their heads with barkcloth headpieces. One barkcloth cloak, now at the Pitt Rivers Museum, Oxford University, was collected on Cook's second voyage. A later example, now in the Peabody Museum of Archaeology and Ethnology, Harvard University, was collected in 1904 by Alexander Agassiz. A belt of turtleshell plates encircled by lengths of barkcloth was collected by H.M.S. *Topaze* in 1868 and is now in the British Museum (fig. 13).

The rarity of barkcloth suggests that barkcloth-covered figures—possibly receptacles for ancestral spirits—might have been considered higher-status substitutes for wood figures. Barkcloth constructions are three-dimensional sculptures with an internal framework of reeds or some other plant material. This framework was completely covered with white barkcloth, which was then decorated with designs similar to Rapa Nui body painting and tattoo (see figs. 18, 19). Only seven barkcloth constructions are known: two headdresses (including cat. no. 38), one hollow, Janus-faced head (cat. no. 27), one human-fish form (cat. no. 26), and three anthropomorphic figures (including cat. nos. 24, 25).

One of the anthropomorphic barkcloth figures, now in the Peabody Museum, Harvard (cat. no. 24), is essentially naturalistic in form. In profile, the face is reminiscent of a bird and shares characteristics with the birdlike profile of the Māori figures known as *manaia*. The body is rounded, and the hands are distinctly human. The back has a well-formed spinal

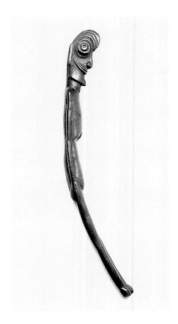
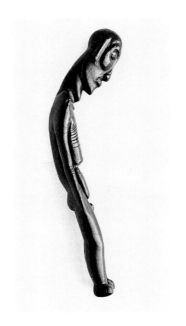
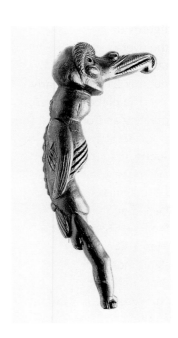

Left: Figure 14. Male figure. 18th–early 19th century. Wood, H. 52 cm (20½ in.). Peter the Great Museum of Anthropology and Ethnology, Russian Academy of Sciences, St. Petersburg

Center: Figure 15. Male figure. 18th–early 19th century. Wood, H. 30 cm (11¾ in.). Peter the Great Museum of Anthropology and Ethnology, Russian Academy of Sciences, St. Petersburg

Right: Figure 16. Birdman figure (*tangata manu*). 18th–early 19th century. Wood, H. 33.5 cm (13⅛ in.). Peter the Great Museum of Anthropology and Ethnology, Russian Academy of Sciences, St. Petersburg

column with distinct vertebrae that continue up over the top of the head, as in some Hawaiian figures. In terms of body form and facial decoration, the figure is similar to two wood examples now in the Peter the Great Museum of Anthropology and Ethnology, Russian Academy of Sciences, St. Petersburg (figs. 14, 15), which are two of the three earliest-known Rapa Nui figures to reach Europe. One has no indications of ribs, the other has incised ribs, and both have features also seen in later wood forms. The crescentric relief carving on the head of the ribless figure (fig. 14) is remarkably similar to the face painting on the Peabody barkcloth figure, especially in profile. The body of the companion piece (fig. 15) is similar to that of the Peabody barkcloth figure and, with its incised ribs, can be considered a prototype for the slightly later classic form of *moai kavakava* (see cat. nos. 7–10). The primary differences between the St. Petersburg prototype and the classic form are the well-carved ribs and greater differentiation of the rib cage from the stomach in the latter. The third wood figure in St. Petersburg (fig. 16), a prototype for the classic *tangata manu* (see cat. nos. 4, 5) has well-carved ribs and a well-delineated vertebral column similar to those of *moai kavakava*.

In the two other known human barkcloth figures—a second example from the Peabody Museum (cat. no. 25) and another in the Ulster Museum, Belfast—the head is quite naturalistically proportioned but the body is flat. Indeed, their bodies resemble the flat bodies of the usually female wood images known as *moai papa*. Nevertheless, the Peabody's flat barkcloth figure is clearly male, while the Belfast figure wears the remnants of a loincloth. Thus, although the human barkcloth figures exhibit two distinct body types, naturalistic and flat—forms comparable to the *moai kavakava* and *moai papa* figures, respectively—all three examples appear to be male.

The body proportions of the human barkcloth figures are similar to those of the much larger stone *moai*, with the head constituting about one-third of the total height. The *moai* lack legs altogether, and while the barkcloth figures do have legs, they are de-emphasized and do not seem to affect the overall body proportions because of the way they are bent upward. This raised-knee position is also seen in some wood figures, such as catalogue number 21 and an early example now in the British Museum (fig. 17).

The elaborate decoration of barkcloth figures, which represents body painting and/or tattoos, associates them with high-ranking individuals. Tattoo was widespread in Polynesia and often associated with chiefly or warrior status. The face, neck, torso, back, legs, arms, and the top of the head were all important locations for tattoo designs. Rapa Nui tattooing implements were similar to those found elsewhere in Polynesia—a comb of bird bone lashed at a right angle to a wood handle. The comb was dipped in dye and the implement struck with another stick to insert the pigment into the skin. Men had more tattoos than women, and chiefs, warriors, and other high-status individuals had more tattoos than commoners. The body decoration on the human barkcloth figures corresponds to historically documented Rapa Nui tattooing, such as the face and neck designs of Juan Tepano, recorded in an undated carte de visite by Tahitian photographer Madame Hoare (fig. 18) and illustrated in a drawing by Swedish ethnologist Hjalmar Stolpe (fig. 19), who traveled in the Pacific in the 1880s. The elaborate body tattoo patterns on the barkcloth figures indicate that they probably represent men of rank, while the head painting patterns may be associated with the birdman religion, symbolically linking the wearer with the god Makemake.

Some barkcloth figures have inserts of heavy, twisted barkcloth at the back of the neck, which could have been used to suspend the figure around the neck of the owner. Indeed, the barkcloth figures might have been worn by the *ariki mau* in the same way that wood figures were worn around the necks of lower-status individuals at feasts and other ceremonial occasions. This is another indication that the barkcloth figures represent high-status versions of the wood figures.

In his ethnographic account based on fieldwork in the 1930s, Alfred Métraux noted that house entrances on Rapa Nui were guarded by wood or barkcloth images representing lizards or other zoomorphic creatures.[6] A number of wood lizard figures (cat. nos. 16–20) and one zoomorphic barkcloth figure (cat. no. 26) exist today. It is possible that the zoomorphic barkcloth figure—which combines animal and human traits—was used as a house protector by a chief such as the *ariki mau,* while wood lizards or other zoomorphic images were used by lower-ranking individuals.

Although we have no information about the functions of the two barkcloth headpieces now in the Peabody Museum (see cat. no. 38), such objects would have been appropriate head cover for a high-status person and added to that person's sacred *mana*. The importance of color and material for a head covering is apparent in the top knots (*pukao*) of the stone *moai,* which are red, the sacred Polynesian color. Only individuals of the highest social rank wore barkcloth headdresses. Other high-status individuals wore feather headdresses—coiled circlets of plant fiber usually covered with iridescent black rooster feathers, some of which projected in elaborate crescents.[7]

6. Métraux 1940, p. 265.
7. Forster 1986, p. 324.

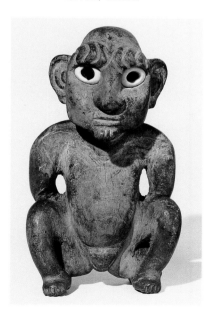

Figure 17. Male figure. 18th–early 19th century. Wood, H. 17 cm (6¾ in.). British Museum, London

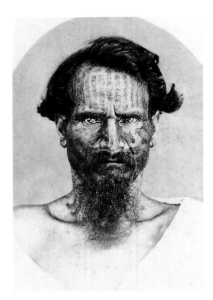

Figure 18. Carte de visite (detail). 1870s. Photograph of Juan Tepano by Madame Hoare. Collection of Mark and Carolyn Blackburn

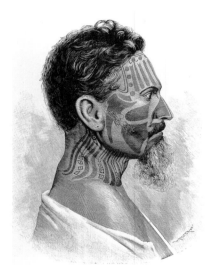

Figure 19. Profile view of Juan Tepano's face. Engraving, after the drawing by Hjalmar Stolpe (1841–1905), 1883–85. In Stolpe, "Über die Tätowirung der Oster-Insulaner," in *Abhandlungen und Berichte des Königlischen, Zoologischen und Antropologisch-Ethnographischen Museums zu Dresden* 8, no. 6 (1899), fig. 5

Barkcloth or feather headdresses were worn on special occasions by chiefs and other prominent individuals as symbols of their rank.

Even more enigmatic is the barkcloth Janus-faced head now in the New Brunswick Museum, Saint John, Canada (cat. no. 27). This hollow object—8 inches high with two faces each painted in black and red—is reminiscent of the Janus-faced staffs (*ua*; cat. nos. 46, 47) and the Janus-faced painted dance paddle ('*ao*; cat. no. 42) now in the Department of Anthropology, Smithsonian Institution, Washington, D.C. Indeed, this hollow barkcloth head, with an interior space of approximately 5 inches, might have been placed over the head of an *ua* to indicate the exalted rank of its owner.

OTHER SCULPTURAL FORMS

Carved-wood breast ornaments (*rei miro*) were worn at feasts and ceremonies by people of high rank. They are similar in form to gorgets and wood crescents worn on mourning costumes from the Society Islands and to chest ornaments depicted on Austral Island sculptures. Other, more realistic wood carvings—from turtles to human feet to *tahonga* (rounded objects resembling eggs or coconuts and sometimes carved with heads; see frontispiece)—were also worn around the neck as ornaments.

Staffs and short clubs (*ua* and *paoa*) served as both weapons and symbols of authority (see cat. nos. 45–47). Adorned with carved Janus-faced heads with eyes of inlaid obsidian and bird bone, they are related in form and function to similar objects from the Marquesas and Aotearoa. *Paoa* were used in hand-to-hand fighting and are directly comparable to Māori hand clubs (*patu*). However, Rapa Nui spears, with their obsidian points, were weapons unique in Polynesia. The points, called *mata'a*, were carefully flaked and hafted to 1½-to-2½-meter-long shafts of light wood.

Wood tablets (*kohau rongorongo*) from Rapa Nui incised with glyphs are thought to be objectified representations of intoned texts. Specialists (*tangata rongorongo*) apparently handled the boards—now considered by many to be mnemonic devices—while reciting genealogies and oral traditions at important festivals and feasts. (Similar specialists were also found in Mangareva, although they did not use tablets as memory aids.) The boards made it possible to transform a transient text into a material object that could retain a measure of sanctity after the oral rendition was completed. It is likely that the tablets are post-European in origin. While there have been efforts to decode it, the exact meaning of *rongorongo* remains a mystery.

ARTISTIC CONVENTIONS

In addition to the backbone and ribs, other particularly notable features of Rapa Nui figures include the hands and eyes; high foreheads; overhanging brows; bulbous cheeks; straight, vertically elongated

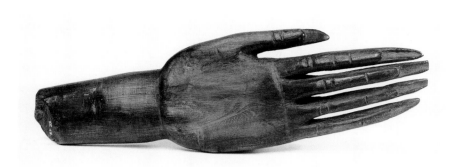

Figure 20. Hand. 18th century. Wood, L. 31 cm (12¼ in.). British Museum, London

noses with flaring nostrils; and, usually, straight, horizontal lips. Well-defined hands must have been important in various contexts. A realistic and elegantly carved hand was collected by Mahine during Cook's visit to Rapa Nui and given to Johann Reinhold Forster, a naturalist on the voyage, who subsequently donated it to the British Museum (fig. 20).[8] Graceful hands rendered in low relief appear on many stone *moai* as well as on many *moai papa*. Some male figures, including an example from the Oldman Collection (now in the Otago Museum, Dunedin, New Zealand) also have elegant hands, as do some lizard figures, the bas-relief figures on the heads of *moai kavakava,* and some rock carvings at Orongo (fig. 21). Hands, represented either realistically or with sticks attached as fingers, are also prominent features of the barkcloth figures.

The eyes in Rapa Nui figures are typically inlaid, a characteristic that links them with certain types of images from Hawai'i and New Zealand, whose eyes are inlaid with shell. Elsewhere in East Polynesia, however, images usually do not have inlaid eyes. The eyes of Rapa Nui wood figures are typically made of round pieces of obsidian encircled by rings of bird bone. In the large stone *moai*, red scoria pupils were embedded in white coral eyes and inset into the eye sockets. The ritual of placing the eyes in the sockets—thus opening the eyes—was an important step in preparing the figure for a ceremony. It is likely that the eyes were only placed in the figures during ceremonies and were removed once the rites were complete. This would account for the fact that only a few eyes have been recovered from archaeological contexts. Many early wood figures are missing one or both eyes, and it is possible that the eyes were removed in order to deconsecrate the figures, thus making them available for trade to passing ships. All five known barkcloth figures have separate

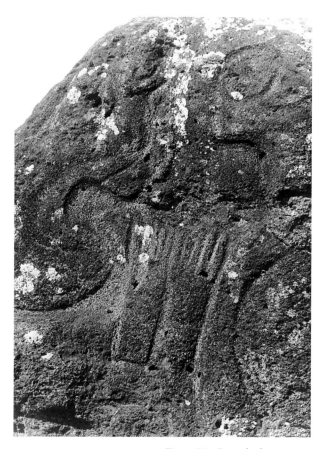

Figure 21. Petroglyphs at Orongo depicting human hands.

8. Ibid., p. 333.

39

9. Métraux 1940, p. 403.

inlaid eyes made of stiff round or oval disks that are covered with white barkcloth with the pupils painted black.

Eyebrows emphasized the importance of the eyes in Rapa Nui figures. In the stone *moai,* the eyebrows are carved as a straight, overhanging ridge forming a frame into which its sacred eyes were set during ceremonies. Eyebrows on wood images are shown as elongated crescents with a central ridge, elaborated with incised chevrons. Barkcloth figures also have eyebrows, modeled in relief. In the unpainted dance paddles (*rapa;* cat. nos. 43, 44), abstract eyebrows indicate the face of an ancestor or god. Along with some indication of earlobes, they were often all that was necessary to convey the essence of human or humanlike form.

The mouth, and especially the lips, of Rapa Nui figures are usually straight and horizontal. Those of the stone figures are closed and pouting. Some wood figures also have well-carved closed lips that are either horizontal or curve slightly upward. The Janus-faced *ua* and *paoa* have similar lips, as do the faces on *rei miro.* The lips of many *moai kavakava,* however, are open, revealing incised teeth, although the primary emphasis is on the lips themselves. In later *moai kavakava* the mouth is emphasized more, the lips are less carefully carved, and the teeth given greater prominence.

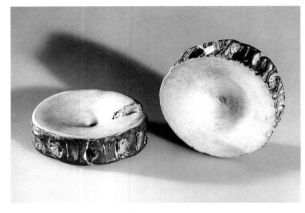

Figure 22. Earplugs. 19th century. Shark vertebrae, D. 4 cm (1 ½ in.). Museum für Völkerkunde Vienna

Well-carved ears are another characteristic of most Rapa Nui figures. Many stone figures have elongated ears, while the staffs (*ua*) have elongated side pieces that represent ears. Early wood figures of all types have carved ears that are sometimes adorned with representations of the ornaments formerly found in the ears of the Rapa Nui, who made enlarged slits in their artificially elongated ears for the insertion of bone earplugs (fig. 22). In *moai kavakava,* earlobes are sometimes carved away from the sides of the face, like appendages. By contrast, the barkcloth figures either have no ears or ears made of stiffened barkcloth or red trade cloth, possibly added at a later date.

THE PERFORMING ARTS

In addition to the island's diverse sculptural traditions, the performing arts have always played a central role in Rapa Nui culture. On Rapa Nui, as elsewhere in Polynesia, these arts were devoted to the worship of ancestors and gods, status validation, entertainment, and, sometimes, social criticism. Texts constituted the essential component of all presentations. Formalized into poetry, they were recited rhythmically and melodically and were visually enhanced by dance. Rapa Nui stories and genealogical recitations were sometimes accompanied by the creation of a series of string figures (cat's cradle) or through the use of objects such as dance paddles ('ao and *rapa*) or incised tablets (*kohau rongorongo*). According to Métraux, each *rongorongo* sign corresponded to a number of words.[9] This is similar in conception to Polynesian dance, in which individual movement

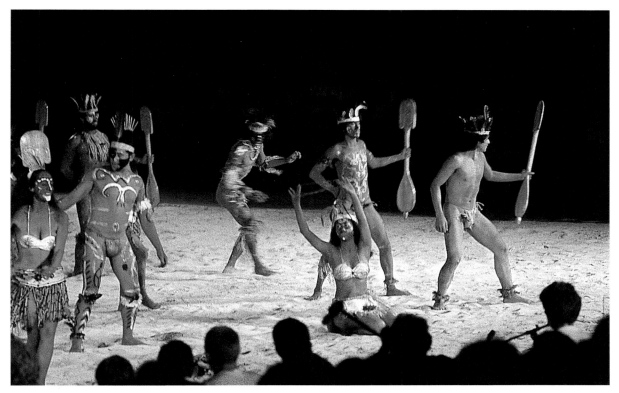

Figure 23. Rapa Nui dancers at the Pacific Festival of Art, Tahiti, 1985, including performers with dance paddles and string figures.

motifs of the hands and arms can be used to allude to, or to interpret, a number of words or concepts. Dance movements, *rongorongo,* or string figures, however, cannot be "read" in the same manner as a written text and do not have meaning without the oral recitation they accompany.

Oratory, music, and dance, composed and performed in both traditional and modern styles for local, national, and international events, remain vigorous on Rapa Nui (fig. 23). Although Rapa Nui was best known in the nineteenth and twentieth centuries for its material objects, it is likely that the featured creative arts of the island in the twenty-first century will be poetry, music, and dance, enhanced by the body decorations and costumes of the performers.

1. Head of a Stone Figure (*moai*)

From the site of Ahu O'Pepe
12th–17th century
Volcanic tuff; H. 47 in. (119.4 cm)
Department of Anthropology, Smithsonian Institution, Washington, D.C.

1. For an account of the collection of this *moai*, see Jo Anne Van Tilburg's essay in this volume.

The quintessential images of Easter Island art are the monumental stone figures, or *moai*. Between roughly A.D. 1100 and the mid-1600s, Rapa Nui artists carved nearly nine hundred of these distinctive figures, which represent ancestral chiefs. Chiefs were believed to be descended directly from the gods—while alive they embodied divine power and after death they were frequently honored as divine ancestors. The focal points of diverse ritual activities, *moai* were normally erected on coastal temple platforms (*ahu*) where they faced inland, keeping watch over the community.

Although it flourished for more than half a millennium, the *moai* tradition was already in decline when the first Europeans arrived at Easter Island in the 1700s. Early explorers reported many *moai* still standing, but by the mid-nineteenth century all of them had fallen as a result of warfare or neglect. Many have since been reerected by archaeologists.

Virtually all *moai* on Easter Island remain in situ. This imposing head, collected by an American expedition in 1886, is one of only a half dozen examples in the West. It was one of seven *moai* associated with the temple Ahu O'Pepe.[1] Carved from volcanic tuff in the main quarry at Rano Raraku, it originally formed part of a figure that stood roughly 8 feet (2.4 m) high, making it among the smaller of the island's stone images. Pitted by centuries of wind and rain, its surface originally would have been smoothly polished.

An elegant and imposing expression of chiefly authority, this head—with its robust brow, aquiline nose, and strong chin—displays the archetypal stylistic features of the *moai* tradition. The high-set ears show the bulbous, artificially extended earlobes characteristic of both Rapa Nui men and women until the late nineteenth century, when the practice was discouraged by Christian missionaries. The flattened cranium once might have supported a red stone cylinder (*pukao*) representing an elaborate coiffure or headdress. During rituals, white coral eyes with pupils of obsidian or red scoria were placed in the eye sockets, awakening the divine power of the ancestral chief for the benefit of the community.

From the site of Ahu O'Pepe

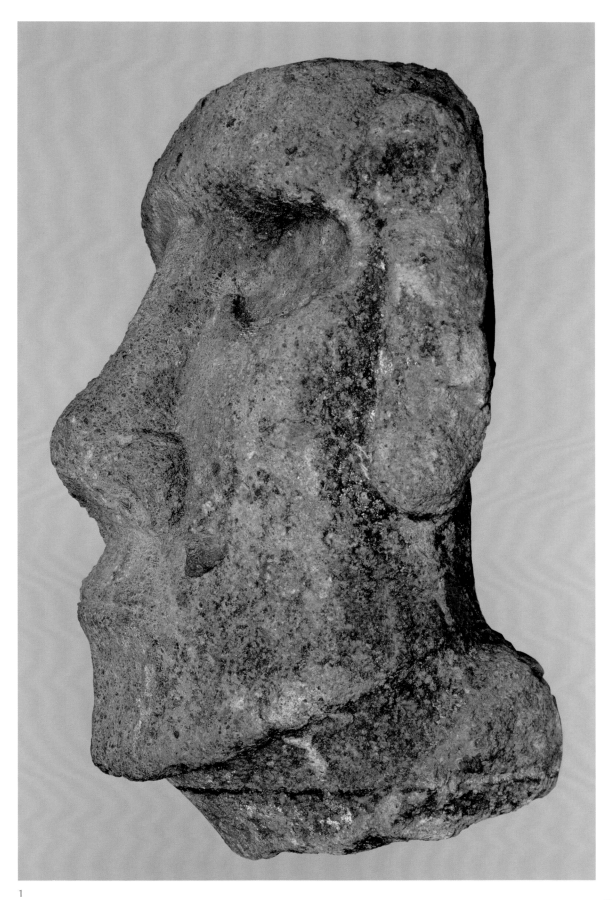

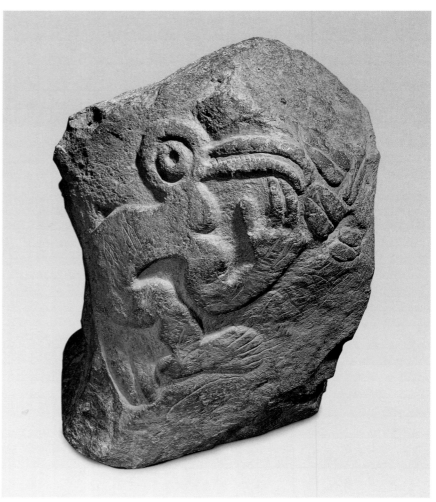

BIRDMAN PETROGLYPHS

2. Birdman Image (*tangata manu*)

Probably from the site of Mata Ngara at Orongo village
15th–19th century
Basalt; H. 18½ in. (47 cm)
Peabody Museum of Archaeology and Ethnology, Harvard University, Cambridge, Massachusetts;
Gift of Alexander Agassiz

3. Double Birdman Image (*manu piri*)

Probably from the site of Mata Ngara at Orongo village
15th–19th century
Basalt; W. 34½ in. (87.6 cm)
Peabody Museum of Archaeology and Ethnology, Harvard University, Cambridge, Massachusetts;
Gift of Alexander Agassiz

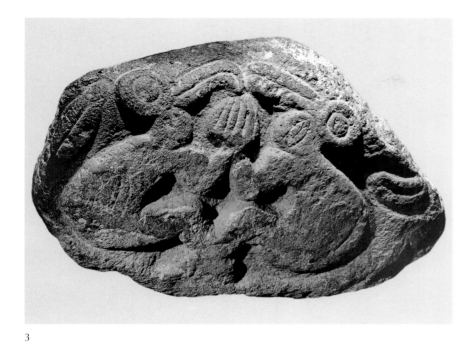

3

Although the exact provenance of these two works is not recorded, their imagery, material, and patina indicate that they almost certainly come from the ceremonial center of Orongo. Representing the creator god Makemake in his manifestation as *tangata manu,* or birdman, they probably once formed part of the dramatic basalt outcrop known as Mata Ngara, where numerous similar images occur.

Orongo was the focus of the annual birdman rites, which centered around a ritualized egg hunt that determined political leadership of Easter Island. The egglike forms of the rocks at Mata Ngara might have motivated Rapa Nui artists to adorn them with the hundreds of birdman images that cover nearly their entire surface. Carved primarily in low relief, the images depict the birdman as a fantastic hybrid—a crouching bird-headed human with wide staring eyes. The hooked beaks and pronounced throat pouches of the images indicate that their heads are that of the *makohe,* or frigate bird (*Fregata minor*). Identified by Rapa Nui in the early twentieth century as images of Makemake, the birdman carvings may also represent the individual birdmen who served as his earthly representatives each year.[1] If so, the approximately four hundred birdman images at the site imply that the ceremonies lasted from sometime in the mid-fifteenth century until the last recorded birdman rites in the 1860s, dates that roughly correspond with those proposed by some archaeologists.

Rendered in low relief with an enlarged frigate bird head, catalogue number 2 displays the classic features of Mata Ngara birdman images. The head surmounts a tense compressed body whose position evokes that of a chick within its egg poised to break from the shell. To the right of the central figure are several stylized vulvas (*komari*), smaller examples of which are superimposed on the figure's body. The most numerous petroglyph motif at Orongo, *komari* might have been carved as part of the adolescent initiation ceremonies also held at the site.[2]

Catalogue number 3 represents an unusual variant on the birdman form. Here two figures are joined at the hands and feet to form a double image known as the *manu piri,* the precise significance of which is unknown.

1. Routledge 1919, p. 263; Métraux 1940, p. 341.
2. Métraux 1940, p. 313; Van Tilburg 1994, pp. 57–58.

BIRDMAN FIGURES

4. Birdman Figure (*tangata manu*)

19th century
Wood; H. 13 in. (33 cm)
American Museum of Natural History, New York

5. Birdman Figure (*tangata manu*)

19th century
Wood, obsidian, and bone; H. 13¼ in. (33.5 cm)
Springfield Science Museum, Springfield, Massachusetts

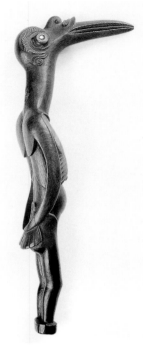

5

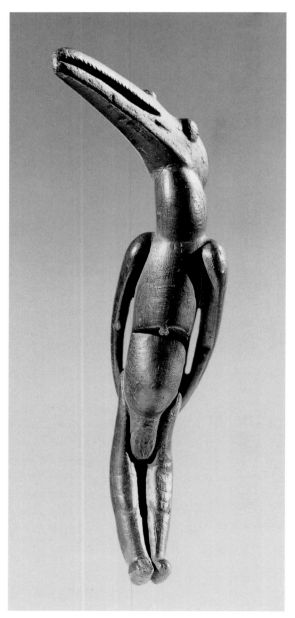

4

Like the petroglyphs of Orongo, Easter Island's wood birdman images almost certainly represent the god Makemake. Wood images of Makemake are reported to have been carried during feasts in his honor.[1] Although the form of these images is not recorded, it seems reasonable to suppose that the handful of surviving wood birdman figures may be examples. In contrast to the crouching forms of the birdman petroglyphs (see cat. nos. 2, 3), the wood images depict the figure standing erect with his head tipped back and prominent beak slightly raised.

Catalogue numbers 4 and 5, probably created by different hands several decades apart, are similar in form but show considerable variation in the treatment of surface detail. Long hailed as a masterwork of Rapa Nui sculpture, number 4 is likely the earlier of the two figures. Wood was rare on the island, and carvers frequently adapted their compositions to accommodate the twisted forms of the *toromiro* trees or driftwood with which they worked. Here the artist took full advantage of the natural shape of the branch to create an image whose subtle curves and sinuous rhythm have few equals in Easter Island carving. Surface details are minimized. Lacking the inlays characteristic of other wood figures, the eyes are rendered as smooth convex knobs. There is a mere allusion to the rib cage, a feature that is highly detailed in many Rapa Nui wood figures. Although its smooth surface reflects a minimal aesthetic, this figure is unique in that it bears a number of finely carved inscriptions in the Easter Island script (*rongorongo*). *Rongorongo* was used to record sacred texts, and these inscriptions possibly represent songs or invocations devoted to Makemake.

The treatment of the face and rib cage in catalogue number 5 is more typical of the surviving corpus of Easter Island wood sculpture and exemplifies the greater detail made possible by steel tools. Collected prior to 1858, its unusual imagery depicts a bird's head emerging from beneath a masklike representation of the human face. This distinctive iconography is an inversion of that seen in a similar birdman figure in the British Museum, whose human head is surmounted by a birdlike mask. The composite nature of the head in both instances may reflect the spiritual transformation of the victorious chief in the annual birdman competition from a human being to the earthly embodiment of Makemake. As with many Rapa Nui wood carvings collected during the nineteenth century, the phalluses of both figures have been removed to satisfy Victorian notions of propriety.

1. Geiseler 1883, pp. 31–33.

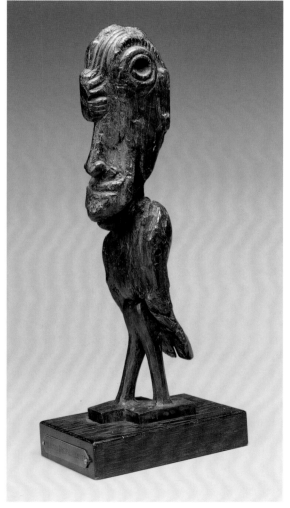

6

6. Birdman Figure (*tangata manu*)

19th century; legs and base, France, late 19th–early 20th century
Wood; H. 11⅜ in. (29 cm)
Helios Trust Collection; courtesy Francesco Pellizzi

In the late nineteenth and early twentieth centuries, wood sculpture from Easter Island enjoyed considerable popularity among European artists and collectors and became an important influence on the Surrealists and other artists. Among the earliest and most influential accounts of Easter Island art was the book *L'Île de Pâques et ses mystères,* published by Parisian collector Charles Stéphen-Chauvet. One of the most striking works in Stéphen-Chauvet's study is this unusual birdman figure. Originally owned by the artist and writer Pierre Loti, who collected it when he visited the island in 1872,[1] the figure is a reversal of the classic birdman image, depicting a human head on the body of a bird. Whether the figure represents Makemake, as do other birdman images, or another supernatural being is unclear.

The distinctive legs and base of the originally limbless figure were added by Loti, creating a composite sculpture whose imagery anticipates the later work of the Surrealists. The original form of the figure strongly resembles the zoomorphic barkcloth effigy seen in catalogue number 26. In both instances, an enlarged head decorated with concentric lines, which may represent facial painting, sits atop a reduced body with a flattened transverse tail.

1. Stéphen-Chauvet 1935, pl. 43, nos. 114–55.

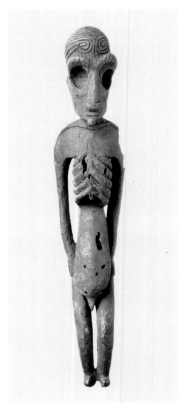

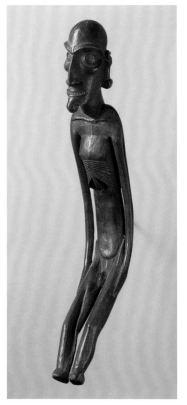

7

8

RIBBED FIGURES
(*moai kavakava*)

7. Male Figure

18th–early 19th century
Wood; H. 10¼ in. (26 cm)
Department of Anthropology, Smithsonian Institution, Washington, D.C.

8. Male Figure

Early 19th century
Wood; H. 14¼ in. (36.2 cm)
Collection of Mark and Carolyn Blackburn

9. Male Figure

19th century
Wood, obsidian, and bone; H. 15 in. (38.1 cm)
Indiana University Art Museum, Bloomington; Raymond and Laura Wielgus Collection

10. Male Figure

19th century
Wood and sealing wax; H. 17 in. (43.2 cm)
Peabody Essex Museum, Salem, Massachusetts

Moai kavakava—literally "image with ribs"—are the most abundant of Easter Island's diverse *moai miro*, or wood images. According to some accounts, these gaunt, at times almost skeletal, male figures represent the spirits of the dead.[1] These spirits, some of whom were likely venerated as ancestors, were believed to take the form of emaciated humans with protruding bones.[2] Indeed, with their grimacing faces, prominent rib cages, and distended abdomens, it seems reasonable to suppose the figures may depict corpses.

In one oral tradition, the first *moai kavakava* are said to have been carved by Tuu-ko-ihu, one of the original settlers, as likenesses of two dangerous spirits, Hitirau and Nuku-te-mango, whom he had encountered while out walking. Tuu-ko-ihu subsequently became a master wood-carver and was believed to have had the power to make the images walk like living beings.[3]

Little is known about the precise functions of *moai kavakava*. One

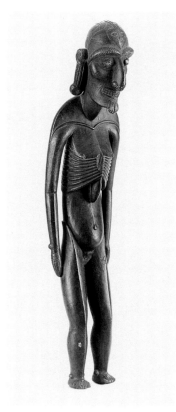

9

10

source reports that their use was restricted to men and that they were worn around the neck as part of festival dress at feasts and other important occasions.[4] The backs of most examples bear a single hole that might have been used to suspend them in this way.

The heads of *moai kavakava* exemplify the distinctive stylistic features of Easter Island's anthropomorphic wood images, including bald crania, prominent brow ridges, and goatee-like beards, as well as artificially extended earlobes. The earlobes are shown with cylindrical ear ornaments representing the actual shark vertebra (*ivi mango*) earplugs worn by the Rapa Nui (see fig. 22). Although Rapa Nui legend tells of a battle between long-eared and short-eared peoples in which the former were annihilated, the practice of lengthening the earlobe was widespread at the time of first contact and is also seen in the stone *moai* (see cat. no. 1).[5]

The crania of *moai kavakava* and other wood images bear a variety of designs, ranging from geometric motifs (cat. no. 7) to birds (see cat. no. 15) and fantastic animals that resemble some of the crouching zoomorphic figures (see cat. nos. 21, 22). Compare, for example, the motif on the head of catalogue number 10 with the similar three-dimensional image in number 22. Although it has been suggested that these cranial images represent tattoos, they do not strongly resemble Rapa Nui head tattoos known from historical sources.

Stylistically, *moai kavakava* vary considerably, suggesting that they were created by a number of artists over a lengthy period of time. Although precise dating is not possible, catalogue numbers 7 and 8 are probably among the earlier examples. The weathered surface of number 7 indicates that it was already of considerable age when collected in 1840.[6] The wide shallow eyes (now missing their inlays), schematic treatment of the body, and lack of surface detail all suggest that it was made with stone tools. In number 8, as in numbers 4 and 18, the artist has adapted the composition to fit the form of the available raw material. The use of small, eccentrically shaped pieces of wood by Rapa Nui carvers during the early contact period is recorded by several observers. The less-detailed treatment of the head and relatively matte surface also imply an early date.

The more regular forms, highly polished surfaces, and intricate details of catalogue numbers 9 and 10 indicate that they probably date to the early to mid-nineteenth century. Each reflects a distinct artistic hand. Number 9 represents the classic expression of the *moai kavakava* image. Strong facial features, robust limbs, and a commanding presence belie its gaunt stomach and skeletal rib cage, creating a corpselike image that paradoxically exudes an overwhelming vitality. Its eyes exhibit the characteristic bone and obsidian inlays of Easter Island wood sculpture. With its markedly stooped stance, pinched face, and great emphasis on the rib cage and clawlike breastbone, number 10, by contrast, presents a more realistic portrayal of old age and death. The eyes are inlaid with red sealing wax obtained from a passing ship.

1. Métraux 1940, p. 260.
2. Ibid., p. 319.
3. Routledge 1919, p. 270; Métraux 1940, pp. 260–61.
4. Routledge 1919, p. 269.
5. Although the practice was discouraged by missionaries in the 1860s, a number of individuals with lengthened ears survived into the early twentieth century. Ibid., p. 203.
6. This image was actually collected by the U.S. Exploring Expedition in New Zealand, where it had been taken earlier by an unknown European or American vessel.

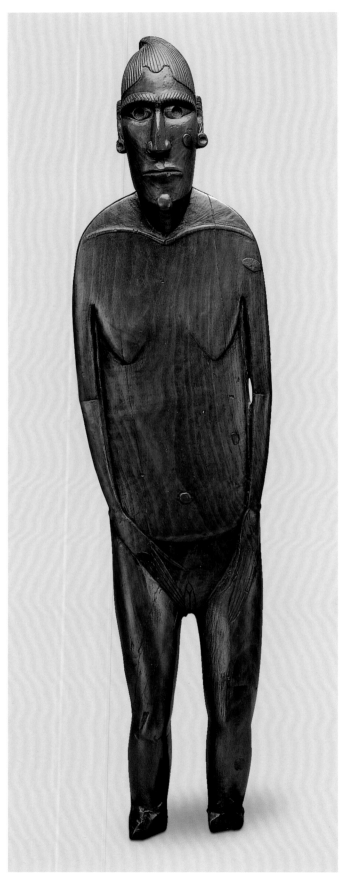

FEMALE FIGURES
(*moai papa*)

11. Female Figure

19th century
Wood; H. 24 in. (61 cm)
Collection of Faith-dorian Wright

12. Female Figure

19th century
Wood, glass, and paint; H. 23⅝ in. (60 cm)
The Metropolitan Museum of Art, New York; The Michael
C. Rockefeller Memorial Collection, Bequest of Nelson A.
Rockefeller, 1979
1979.206.1478

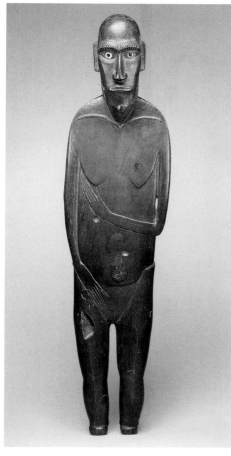

12

Far rarer than their male counterparts, Easter Island's female images (*moai papa*) display a different approach to the human form, with wide, planklike bodies that contrast with their fully modeled heads. Although *moai papa* translates roughly as "flat image," the name may have more profound associations. The term *papa* literally denotes a flat horizontal surface of volcanic rock. However, it may also be an oblique reference to Papa, the female personification of the earth, or "earth mother," who is found in many Polynesian traditions and whom the figures possibly represent.[1]

Like *moai kavakava,* the first *moai papa* images are said to have been made by the carver Tuu-ko-ihu. According to some oral traditions, Tuu-ko-ihu dreamed that he encountered two female spirits, Paapa Ahiro and Paapa Akirangi, who attempted to cover their genitals with their hands (in a manner similar to that depicted in the *moai papa*). On waking, Tuu-ko-ihu created images of the spirits he had seen.[2]

Although indisputably female, *moai papa* also display masculine features, including goatees and, in most instances, bald heads. The significance of this imagery is unknown, but inclusion of such masculine attributes may indicate that the power of the goddesses (or possibly female ancestors) they represent was perceived as equivalent to that of their male counterparts.

Catalogue number 12 presents the classic *moai papa* image, with its strongly flattened body, bald head, and somewhat heavy facial features. The cavity in the right leg and numerous wood plugs indicate that this may be a relatively early example created before large unblemished blocks of wood became available.

A more refined image, catalogue number 11 has realistic hair and delicate facial features that lend it a serene and graceful presence. Reputedly owned by the Surrealist painter Wolfgang Paalen, it embodies many of the features that attracted twentieth-century European artists to African and Oceanic art—the expression of an unfamiliar aesthetic that nevertheless possesses a universal appeal.

1. Routledge 1919, pp. 269–70.
2. Métraux 1940, pp. 260–61; Routledge 1919, pp. 269–70.

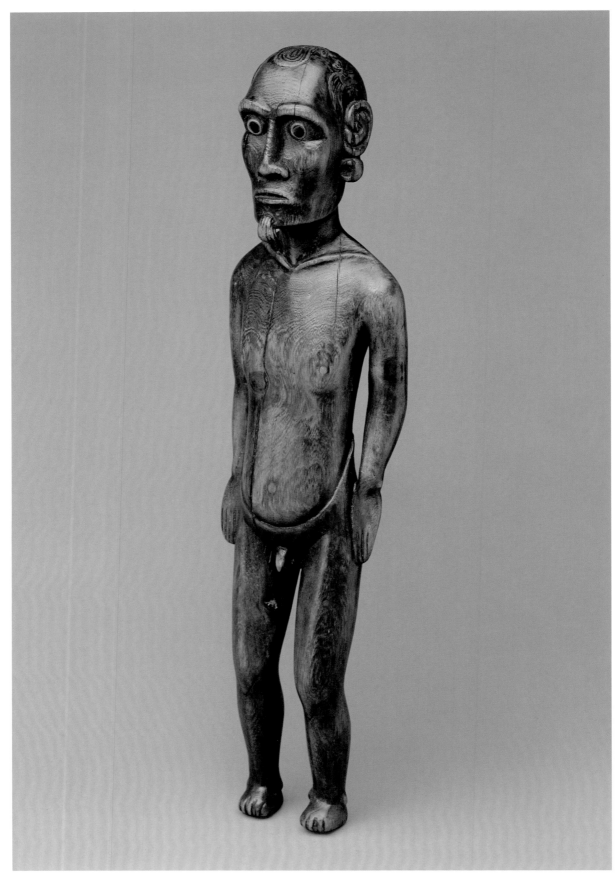

NATURALISTIC MALE FIGURES
(*moai tangata*)

13. Male Figure

19th century
Wood, obsidian, and bone; H. 16 in. (40.6 cm)
The Metropolitan Museum of Art, New York; Gift of Faith-dorian and
Martin Wright, in honor of Livio Scamperle, 1984
1984.526

14. Male Figure

19th century
Wood, obsidian, bone, and trade cloth; H. 9⅛ in. (23.2 cm)
Collection of Mark and Carolyn Blackburn

15. Fragmentary Figure

19th century
Wood and sealing wax; H. 7⅛ in. (18.1 cm)
Collection of Mark and Carolyn Blackburn

In contrast with the skeletal *moai kavakava*, the *moai tangata* depict well-nourished, at times slightly corpulent, male figures. Possibly representing family ancestors, some of these images, although conventionalized, may be individual portraits.[1] Among the island's wood sculptures, the *moai tangata*—with their enlarged heads, strictly frontal orientation, prominent stomachs, and arms extended down the sides of their bodies—bear the closest formal resemblance to the stone *moai*.

The erect stance, robust body, and more naturalistic physiognomy of catalogue number 13 are characteristic features of *moai tangata*. What at first appears to be hair is actually a group of three low-relief images depicting fishlike creatures with human heads and long flowing beards. Similar "fishmen" motifs appear on the crania of many *moai tangata* and are virtually identical to petroglyphs at a number of sites on the island. It is possible they represent mythical shark-human spirits known as *nuihi*.[2]

The robust, compact body and unusual proportions of catalogue number 14 suggest that this figure depicts a dwarf, possibly a specific individual. While the right eye displays the typical bone and obsidian inlays, the pupil of the left is made from trade cloth. As obsidian is abundant on the island, the use of the more valuable cloth probably represented a conscious decision on the part of the artist to attempt to appropriate some of the perceived power of Europeans through inclusion of this imported material.

The fragmentary figure in catalogue number 15 exhibits a notable departure from the conventions of the *moai tangata* form. The strict symmetry of Easter Island sculpture is broken, as the subject gazes over its right shoulder while its surviving left forearm extends behind

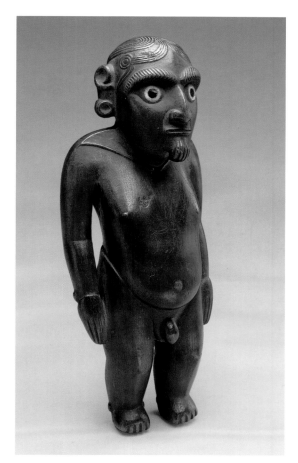

14

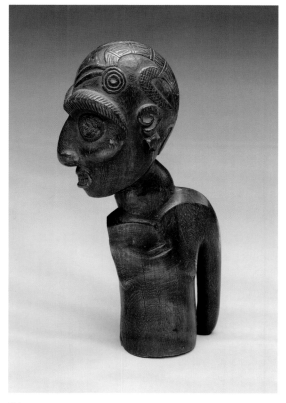

1. Routledge 1919, pp. 270–71.
2. See Lee 1992, pp. 39–40, 164.
3. Van Tilburg 1994, p. 176; 1992, p. 31.

the small of the back. The eyes are inlaid with red sealing wax. The most striking element in the composition are the two large bird forms that adorn the cranium. Similar bird images are found on many wood figures, including number 14, and also occur as petroglyphs. Many depict the frigate bird (*makohe*), which is thought to have served as an emblem of the dominant Miru lineage.[3] If so, these particular *moai tangata,* like the stone figures, may be images of ancestral chiefs.

LIZARDMAN FIGURES (*moko*)

16. Lizardman Figure

19th century
Wood and bone; L. 15½ in. (39.4 cm)
Collection of Arman and Corice Arman

17. Lizardman Figure

19th century
Wood; L. 13½ in. (34.3 cm)
Peabody Museum of Archaeology and Ethnology, Harvard University, Cambridge, Massachusetts;
Gift of the Heirs of David Kimball

18. Lizardman Figure

19th century
Wood, obsidian, and bone; L. 15 in. (38.1 cm)
Collection of Raymond and Laura Wielgus

19. Lizardman Figure

19th century
Wood, obsidian, and bone; L. 19¼ in. (48.9 cm)
The Metropolitan Museum of Art, New York; Rogers Fund, 1995
1995.416

20. Lizardman Figure

19th century
Wood; L. 5⅝ in. (14.3 cm)
Collection of Mark and Carolyn Blackburn

Among the most distinctive of Easter Island's wood images are the gracefully curving *moko,* or lizardmen. *Moko* literally translates as "lizard," but the lizardmen are composite figures, with the heads and tails of lizards, the fan-like tail feathers of birds, and crouching human bodies whose prominent ribs, backbones, and phalluses resemble those of the *moai kavakava.* Although they resemble the island's native lizards (*Cryptoblepharus boutonii*), *moko* probably depict powerful spirits (*akuaku*).

Lizardman images on Easter Island appear to have been intimately associated with the built environment and were involved in the creation, defense, and destruction of dwellings and ceremonial structures. During rites associated with the completion of important houses, possibly those of chiefs, wood

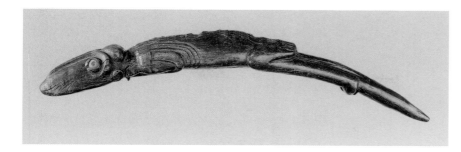

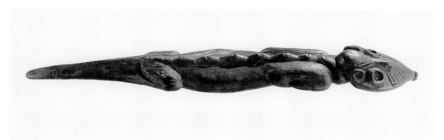

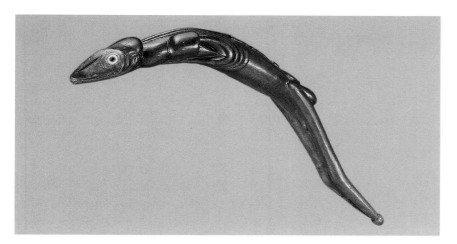

lizardmen were placed on either side of the entrance. The *ariki mau* and a high priest then entered the house and ate a ceremonial first meal.[1] These lizardman images might have protected the threshold from supernatural foes; larger examples were reputedly used as clubs to defend the entrance against human enemies.[2]

Smaller lizardman figures, such as catalogue numbers 17–20, might have been placed at house entrances or suspended from the interior rafters as supernatural guardians. Such images are also said to have been worn as pendants by dancers during feasts, while larger *moko* were carried in the arms and moved rhythmically in time to the dance.[3]

The *moko* presented here reflect five distinct and highly individualistic approaches to the form. The eroded, less polished surfaces and more schematic details of catalogue numbers 16 and 17 suggest that they may be the earliest of the group. Number 16 presents the essential *moko* image: its streamlined head and gently curving body form a relaxed and graceful arc that contrasts with the compact tension of the limbs. The stylized treatment of the nose and eyebrows resembles that seen on the dance paddles (see cat. nos. 42–44), while

1. Routledge 1919, p. 243.
2. Métraux 1940, pp. 169, 265.
3. Geiseler 1883, pp. 32, 48.

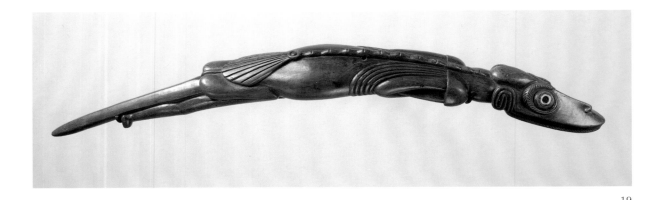

19

4. Métraux 1940, p. 169.

the ribs, spine, hands, and tail feathers are only lightly indicated. In number 17 the carver further simplifies the form, flattening the body and raising the head to create an almost spearlike image. Anatomical detail is minimized, with the limbs and spine reduced to basic shapes and the rib cage and tail feathers omitted altogether, creating a work that emphasizes form over ornamentation.

In its otherworldly lightness and consummate use of the natural form of the wood, number 18 represents perhaps the quintessential expression of the *moko* image. Also likely an early work, its elegant simplified features and beautifully polished, slightly twisted body give it a serene yet animated presence that marks it as a masterwork of Rapa Nui sculpture.

Number 19 is a particularly accomplished example of the great efflorescence of Easter Island wood carving in the first half of the nineteenth century. The exquisitely detailed face and body reflect the greater precision made possible by steel tools. Its wide staring eyes and delicate humanlike nose give it a lively quality that contrasts with the more rigidly stylized features of other *moko*.

In both form and detail, number 20 represents a highly idiosyncratic expression of the *moko* image. Unlike the sleek, upward-curving forms more typical of the *moko* tradition, its robust rounded body and raised head and tail produce a downward curve reminiscent of the shape of the *rei miro* (see cat. nos. 33–36). The anthropomorphic head that emerges from its side also resembles the terminal heads of the *rei miro* gorgets. Stylistically, the work is so closely related to another wood image—now in the Pitt Rivers Museum, Oxford University, and thought to depict a Polynesian rat—that the two may be by the same carver. In addition to lizards, figures of rats were among the protective images placed at house entrances, and it is possible this lizard and rat represent such supernatural guardians.[4]

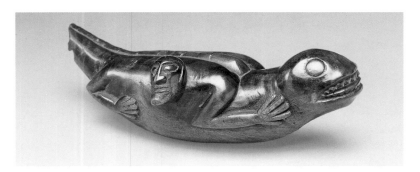

CROUCHING ZOOMORPHIC FIGURES

21. Crouching Figure

19th century
Wood; L. 6½ in. (16.5 cm)
Peabody Essex Museum, Salem,
Massachusetts

22. Crouching Figure

19th century
Wood; L. 8⅝ in. (22 cm)
Peabody Essex Museum, Salem,
Massachusetts

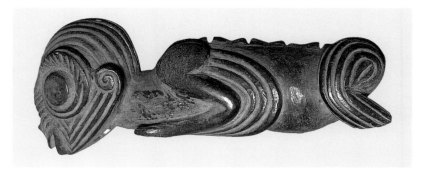

21

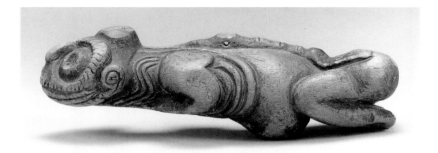

22

Among the most enigmatic of Easter Island wood images are a series of crouching figures whose bodies frequently exhibit both human and animal features. Stylistically, these images are closely related to the lizardmen, sharing the same horizontal orientation, crouching posture, and pronounced rib cages and vertebrae. The figures lack tails, however, and are generally more anthropomorphic. The imagery of the crouching figures is strikingly similar to that of motifs adorning the heads of some *moai kavakava,* such as catalogue number 10. Although it is possible these images depict a distinct category of mythical creature, they may simply be more anthropomorphic variants of the lizardman image and might have had similar functions.

Catalogue number 21 presents a highly stylized, but almost entirely human, image. In form and decoration it closely resembles the male barkcloth figure in number 24, which, although vertically oriented, displays the same crouching posture and transverse bands of decorations on the head. The bands in each case likely represent designs painted on the face, possibly during rituals. The eyes are rendered as integrally carved, low-relief disks whose shallow buttonlike forms are also similar to those of the barkcloth image. The jawline and ears, however, evoke the form of the mouth seen in the lizardmen, indicating the image may represent a being with both human and reptilian characteristics.

The figure in catalogue number 22 exhibits more clearly zoomorphic features. With its strongly prognathous face, avian tail feathers, and pronounced ribs and backbone, it is essentially a tailless and somewhat foreshortened lizardman and may represent a highly anthropomorphic expression of the form. The undulating lines that adorn the neck possibly depict skin folds, but, alternately, they may be representations of the neck tattoos worn by Rapa Nui men, which also appear on the barkcloth images (see cat. nos. 24, 25) and on some stone *moai* (see fig. 12).

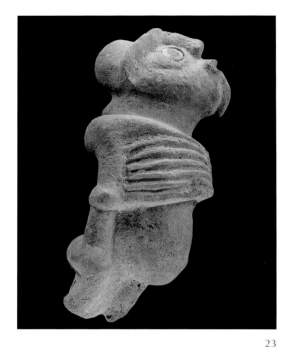

23

23. Stone Figure (*moai maea*)

19th century
Stone; L. 8 in. (20.3 cm)
Peabody Museum of Archaeology and Ethnology, Harvard University,
Cambridge, Massachusetts; Gift of the Heirs of David Kimball

Rapa Nui artists created hundreds of towering *moai,* but smaller stone images are comparatively rare. In form and iconography, many of these more diminutive stone figures resemble the wood images, and they were likely used in similar contexts. The foreshortened body, skeletal features, and prominent belly of catalogue number 23 show close stylistic affinities with the crouching figures (see cat. nos. 21, 22). Its skeletal imagery, however, is highly distinctive in that the rib cage, normally a separate element, is formed from the intersecting fingers of the figure's greatly enlarged hands.

Although tiny in comparison with the larger stone *moai,* number 23 reflects the same creative processes and techniques. Its remarkable state of preservation provides insights into the original appearance of the now heavily eroded *moai.* The figure retains the smooth surface and detailed treatment of the hands and facial features originally present on the large *moai,* and its eyes display distinctive white coral inlays similar to those placed into the eyes of the larger figures during ritual observances. Composed of gray volcanic rock, number 23 is adorned with *kiea,* a red pigment made from mineralized volcanic tuff.[1] The Rapa Nui, like other Polynesian cultures, considered red the most sacred color, and the addition of red pigment to the image probably enhanced its supernatural power (*mana*). At least one large *moai* originally was painted, and others might have been similarly adorned, although their weathered surfaces make that difficult to determine.[2]

1. Métraux 1940, p. 236; Van Tilburg 1994, p. 175.
2. Van Tilburg 1992, p. 40.

BARKCLOTH IMAGES (*manu uru*)

24. Male Figure

19th century
Reeds, barkcloth, wood, and paint; H. 15¾ in. (40 cm)
Peabody Museum of Archaeology and Ethnology, Harvard University, Cambridge, Massachusetts;
Gift of the Heirs of David Kimball

25. Male Figure

19th century
Reeds, barkcloth, wood, and paint; H. 18½ in. (47 cm)
Peabody Museum of Archaeology and Ethnology, Harvard University, Cambridge, Massachusetts;
Gift of the Heirs of David Kimball

Only five examples of Easter Island's fragile and ephemeral barkcloth images (*manu uru*) survive: three seated male figures (including cat. nos. 24, 25), a fishman image (cat. no. 26), and a bifacial head (cat. no. 27).[1] *Manu uru* consist

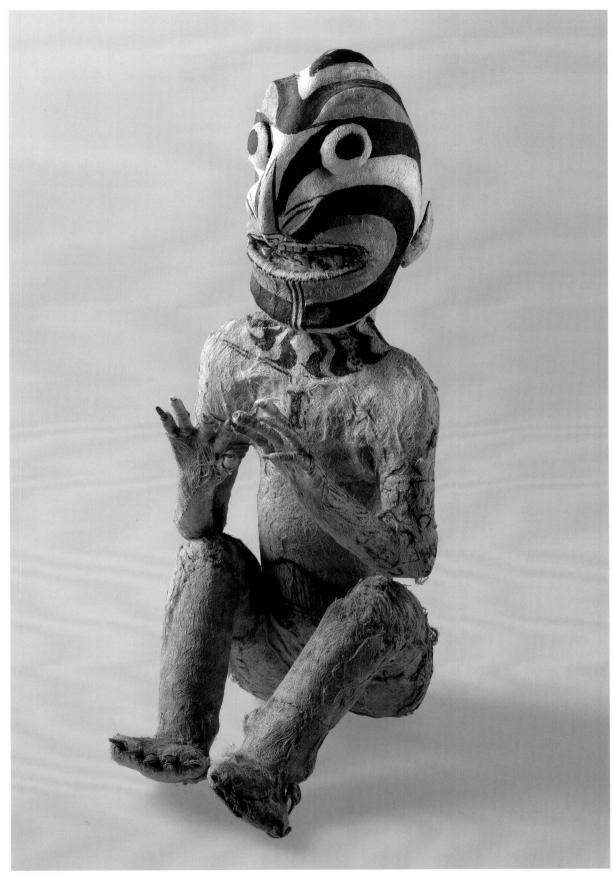

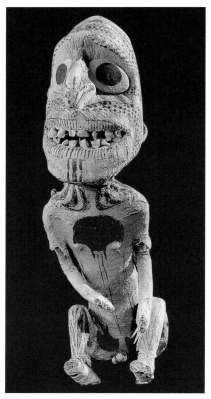

25

of a framework of reeds, wood, and other plant materials overlaid with a skin of fine white barkcloth (*mahute*), which was sewn together with plant fiber using needles of bird or human bone.[2]

Although it is uncertain who fashioned and decorated the images, the barkcloth itself was created by Rapa Nui women, primarily using the soft inner bark of the paper mulberry tree (*Broussonetia papyrifera*). Small strips of bark were collected and then beaten with wood mallets to fuse the individual strips together, forming a clothlike material that was also used for clothing.

The iconography and function of the barkcloth images remain problematic. Some show close stylistic affinities with certain types of wood images, and Adrienne L. Kaeppler suggests that the figures, clad in highly valued white barkcloth, represent high-status versions of their more abundant wood counterparts.[3] Others suggest they may be miniature versions of the large barkcloth effigies described by several early explorers, which were erected at feasts and ceremonies held in honor of a deceased parent (*paina*).[4] Barkcloth figures of lizards or lobsters,[5] like the wood lizard images, are said to have been placed at the entrances of houses to serve as supernatural protectors.[6] If so, such barkcloth guardians were probably used only briefly, possibly as part of consecration rituals, as their fragile materials would have rapidly decayed in an outdoor setting.

Catalogue numbers 24 and 25, both male figures, represent two quite different renditions of the form. Similar in posture to some of the wood figures, such as number 21 (see also fig. 17), the barkcloth images provide a rare glimpse into the intricate tattoos and body painting that formerly adorned the bodies of the Rapa Nui. Comparable in some respects to the *moai tangata*, number 24 presents a robust and vigorous figure whose skin is elaborately decorated. Early explorers reported a number of Rapa Nui whose faces were painted with red and white vertical stripes, and the boldly rendered transverse stripes that adorn the head likely represent similar painted designs.[7] The undulating lines on the throat depict the neck tattoos worn by Rapa Nui men as recorded in historical accounts and early illustrations (see figs. 18, 19). The delicately rendered geometric motifs on the body also represent tattooing. The tattoo patterns on each of the three surviving anthropomorphic images are so distinctive that it is likely they portray specific individuals, who were probably venerated as ancestors.

In comparison with number 24, number 25 presents a gaunt, almost mummylike form whose grimacing mouth and cadaverous quality more closely resemble the *moai kavakava* than the *moai tangata*. The figure bears a typical forehead tattoo pattern (*retu*) with curved lines along the forehead above a series of dots known as *humu* or *puraki*.[8] Its neck tattoos are similar to those of number 24, but the body is decorated with more representational motifs, including the obsidian-tipped spears known as *mata'a,* an indication that the image likely represents a warrior (*paoa*) or war leader (*matatoa*).

1. The third male figure is in the Ulster Museum, Belfast, Northern Ireland. Two additional works—a visorlike headdress (cat. no. 38) and a hatlike object depicting two human faces, both in the Peabody Museum of Archaeology and Ethnology, Harvard University, employ the same technique.
2. Métraux 1940, p. 213. The reeds used in the construction of the figures are the totara (*Scripus californicus*), which grows in the island's crater lakes. Van Tilburg 1994, p. 47.
3. See Kaeppler, this volume.
4. See Métraux 1940, pp. 343–45.
5. Métraux refers to the latter figures as "crayfish." Crayfish are a freshwater species, however, and do not occur on Easter Island. Hence the animals represented by these figures, none of which survive, were probably spiny lobsters, a highly valued prestige food.
6. Métraux 1940, p. 265.
7. Routledge 1919, p. 259.
8. Métraux 1940, p. 241.

26. Fishman (*nuihi?*)

1840s
Reeds, barkcloth, wood, and paint; H. 25 in. (63.5 cm)
New Brunswick Museum, Saint John, Canada

This remarkable fishman is the only zoomorphic image among the surviving corpus of barkcloth figures. Along with catalogue number 27, it was collected in 1843 by the Canadian whaleship *Mary Rait* from a group of Rapa Nui, who swam out to her whaleboats and exchanged the images for pieces of blubber.[1] Although no comparable barkcloth figures exist, the image is nearly identical to two wood examples, one in the British Museum and the other in the Museum für Völkerkunde Berlin. All three have markedly anthropomorphic heads with large round eyes, small noses, and oval mouths opened to expose blunt, humanlike teeth. The eyes on the barkcloth image and one of the wood examples are surrounded by concentric crescents. Likely depicting face painting patterns similar to those of catalogue number 24, they serve as a further indication that the heads of the images are human.

The significance of these human-fish hybrids remains unclear. Like the birdmen and lizardmen, they likely depict supernatural beings whose earthly manifestations combine human and animal characteristics. The fishmen possibly represent *nuihi,* sea spirits believed to take the form of sharks with human heads. However, other *nuihi* images, such as those on the heads of *moai tangata* (see cat. no. 13), generally show the spirits with long flowing beards that are absent in the fishman images. Alternately, the figures may represent seals or sea lions, whose humanlike heads and plump fishlike bodies bear a strong resemblance to those of the fishman images.[2] Seals—almost never seen on Easter Island's shores—might have been fleetingly glimpsed at sea and perceived as the incarnations of supernatural beings.

1. Elliot 1979, p. 168.
2. Seals are almost unknown on Easter Island today, but their bones have been recovered from archaeological contexts. Van Tilburg 1994, p. 50.

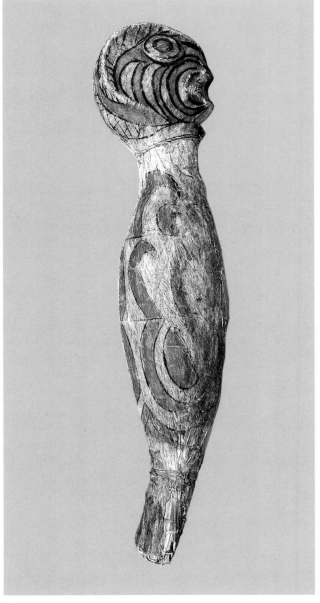

26

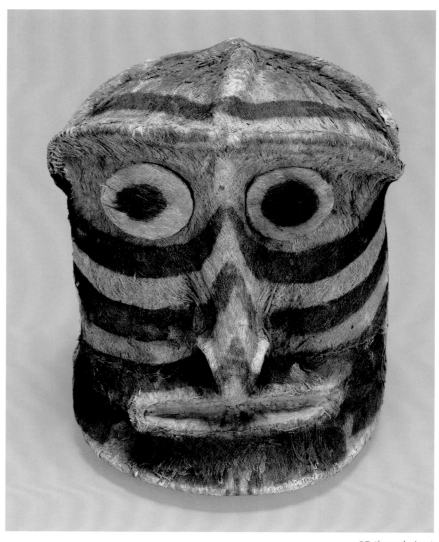

27 (frontal view)

BIFACIAL IMAGES (*moai aringa*)

27. Barkcloth Head

1840s
Reeds, barkcloth, wood, and paint; H. 8 in. (20.3 cm)
New Brunswick Museum, Saint John, Canada

28. Pendant

19th century
Wood and obsidian; H. 3 in. (7.6 cm)
Collection of Mark and Carolyn Blackburn

29. Pendant

19th century
Wood, obsidian, and bone; H. 3¾ in. (9.5 cm)
Peabody Essex Museum, Salem, Massachusetts

Among the most enigmatic expressions of the human form in Rapa Nui art, the *moai aringa* consist of two human faces joined at the back to form a single bifacial, or "Janus-faced," head. *Moai aringa* occur as separate images and also adorn the ends of fighting clubs (*paoa*) and chief's staffs (*ua*), such as catalogue numbers 45–47.

Who or what these images represent is unclear. One Rapa Nui oral tradition, however, may offer a clue. It describes a fight between two chiefs from different districts of the island. The son of one of the rival chiefs, Rau-hiva-aringa-erua ("Twin two faces"), was a legendary warrior born with two faces, one facing forward and the other backward. As followers of the two chiefs met in battle, the rear face saw the warrior Pau-a-ure-vera approaching from behind and asked the front face to turn around and look. When the front face refused, the two began arguing and ignored Pau-a-ure-vera, who slew the two-faced warrior with his spear.[1]

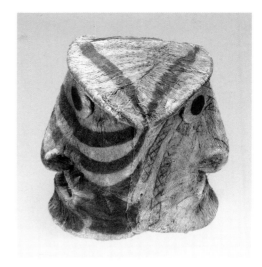

27 (profile view)

The images on each side of the barkcloth head possibly represent the two faces of Rau-hiva-aringa-erua, each adorned with markedly different designs. Rendered in barkcloth, the most perishable of Rapa Nui media, their angular features, pronounced brows, deep-set eyes, tightly compressed mouths, and prominent chins nevertheless display a striking resemblance to the stone *moai*. A bold pattern of upward-curving black and orange stripes dominates the composition of one face, almost entirely covering its surface. The other is more lightly adorned with downward-curving forms whose thin, graceful lines and delicate cross-hatching offset and complement its more robust companion. The careful attention to detail in each face indicates that these designs may represent actual Rapa Nui face paint patterns.

While the function of the barkcloth image is unclear, suspension holes in the wood *moai aringa* suggest that they were worn as pendants. Highly valued prestige ornaments, some wood pendants, such as the *rei miro* gorgets (cat. nos. 33–36), also served as status markers. The heads of the *moai aringa* pendants are similar to those on the staffs (*ua*) carried by male chiefs

1. Routledge 1919, pp. 282–85.

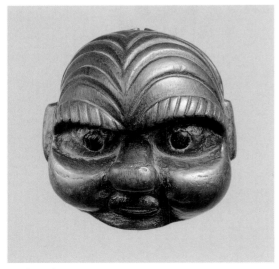

28 (frontal view)

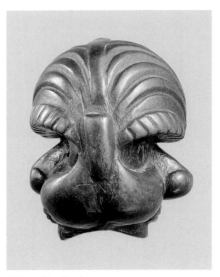

28 (profile view)

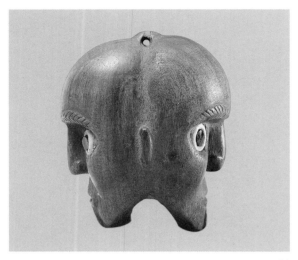
29

(see cat. nos. 46, 47). It is possible, then, that these *moai aringa* pendants are essentially reduced versions of *ua* worn as insignia of chiefly rank.

With its wrinkled brow, bulbous nose and cheeks, and straight, expressionless mouth, catalogue number 28 bears a striking resemblance to the heads on the *ua*. The treatment of the facial features is also closely related to that of a similar pendant in the British Museum. In each case, the face is compressed to emphasize the boldly rendered furrows of the forehead, giving these works an air of intense concentration. Number 29 takes a more naturalistic approach. The smooth forehead, reduced brow ridge, and minimal surface detail lend it a more tranquil, open quality that contrasts with the stern expression of the previous example.

ZOOMORPHIC PENDANTS

30. Pendant

19th century
Wood and obsidian; L. 5 in. (12.7 cm)
Peabody Museum of Archaeology and Ethnology, Harvard University, Cambridge, Massachusetts;
Gift of the Heirs of David Kimball

31. Pendant

19th century
Wood and obsidian; L. 4½ in. (11.4 cm)
Private collection

32. Pendant

19th century
Wood, obsidian, and bone; L. 5½ in. (14 cm)
Collection of Arman and Corice Arman

1. Métraux 1940, p. 235. A belt decorated with turtleshell plates is preserved in the British Museum (see fig. 13).

Rapa Nui art, better known for its blending of human and animal forms, also includes more recognizable zoomorphic images that appear to represent particular species. These three pendants depicting sea turtles and tuna, both highly prized foods, are among the finest expressions of this more realistic tradition within Easter Island sculpture.

Catalogue number 30 depicts a sea turtle (*honu*). Sea turtles are not found on the island today, but they are mentioned in a number of oral traditions and were reportedly captured in former times for their meat and shell.[1] Overall the work is naturalistic, but it also exhibits a markedly minimalist approach to the limbs and shell, which are reduced to their essential forms. Apart from the features of the face, surface detail is eliminated, creating a sleek, streamlined image that appears able to glide effortlessly through the water.

The beaked mouth and forward placement of the nostrils of catalogue number 31 indicate that it likely represents the head of a sea turtle. It is one of a number of closely related turtle head pendants whose form and surface decoration are so similar that, like *rei miro* (see cat. nos. 33–36), they possibly represent a specific category of ornament that indicated the wearer's social rank. Unlike the smooth surfaces of number 30, the artist here expressed almost a horror vacui, adorning virtually the entire work with bold longitudinal grooves. The eyes, rendered as a series of concentric rings surrounding large obsidian inlays, dominate the composition, while the headlike motifs on the cranium appear to be miniature versions of the turtle-head image.

Based on the placement of the fins and gills and its compact, bulletlike form, number 32 likely represents the head of a tuna. Tuna was a rare and highly esteemed delicacy, and its consumption was generally limited to chiefs and other high-status individuals. It is possible, then, that this pendant was worn by a Rapa Nui chief. Its overall shape, prominent longitudinal grooves, and diagonal mouth ornamentation reflect close stylistic affinities with number 31 and suggest that the two served similar functions, perhaps as indicators of the wearer's noble birth.

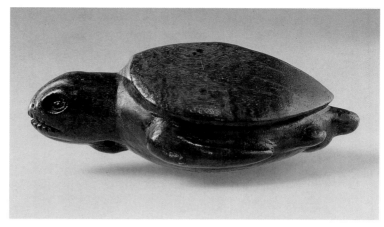

30

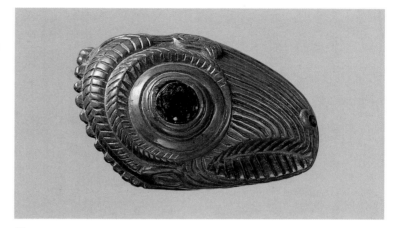

31

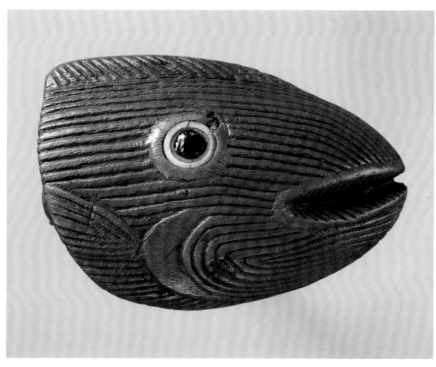

32

GORGETS (*rei miro*)

33. Gorget

19th century
Wood; W. 17¼ in. (43.8 cm)
The Metropolitan Museum of Art, New York; The Michael C. Rockefeller Memorial Collection,
Bequest of Nelson A. Rockefeller, 1979
1979.206.1527

34. Gorget

19th century
Wood, obsidian, and bone; W. 15 in. (38.1 cm)
Collection of Raymond and Laura Wielgus

35. Gorget

19th century
Wood and hair; W. 9⅝ in. (24.4 cm)
Collection of Mark and Carolyn Blackburn

36. Gorget

1860s
Wood, obsidian, and bone; W. 10⅛ in. (25.7 cm)
Collection of Mark and Carolyn Blackburn

1. Routledge 1919, p. 242;
Van Tilburg 1994, p. 103.
2. Métraux 1940, p. 231.

The crescent-shaped gorgets known as *rei miro* were elegant symbols of chiefly authority. Reportedly used primarily by chiefly women, they were worn at feasts and other important occasions, where they served as insignia of noble birth. Meaning literally "necklace of wood," *rei miro* are similar to chiefly ornaments in a number of eastern Polynesian cultures, such as the *taumi* gorgets of Tahiti. Images of *rei miro* appear in the island's rock art and are among the few recognizable symbols portrayed on the *rongorongo* tablets, where it is possible they signify female chiefs. More simplified crescents, also called *rei miro*, were painted on chicken houses to promote fertility, and crescent motifs occur as secondary carvings made on the bodies of *moai* during the late pre-contact period.[1]

Although generally associated with women, *rei miro* also were an important component of the ceremonial attire of the *ariki mau*, who is said to have worn no fewer than six examples at once—two on the chest and two hanging from each shoulder.[2] This use of female ornaments by the island's highest male chief may indicate that the fundamental nature of his divine power and even of his person was perceived as androgynous.

With flat bodies adorned at each end by fully modeled, anthropomorphic heads, catalogue numbers 33 and 34 represent the classic form of the *rei miro* image. The central portion in each case is adorned with a shallow intaglio crescent, whose form echoes and enhances the graceful curve of the ornament. The treatment of the eyes in number 33, perhaps the earlier of the two, is similar to that seen in catalogue numbers 4 and 19. The exquisite detail of the heads in number 34 is particularly refined and reflects the great artistic virtuosity of early-nineteenth-century Rapa Nui carving.

In catalogue number 35, the terminal heads are eliminated, and the image is reduced to its essential form. The crescent, normally intaglio, is here rendered as an openwork element, giving the piece a lighter and surprisingly modern

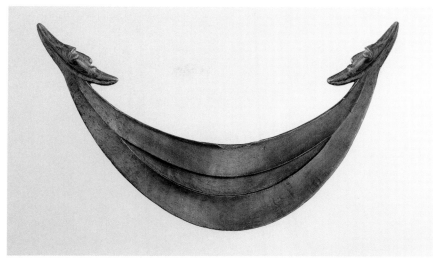

33

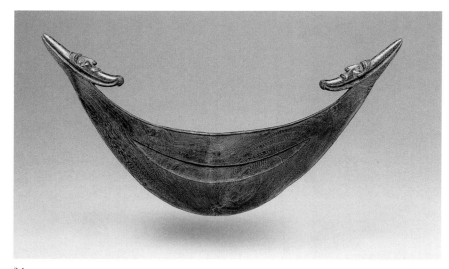

34

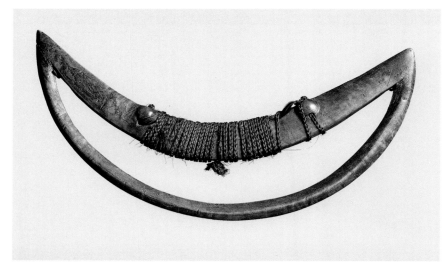

35

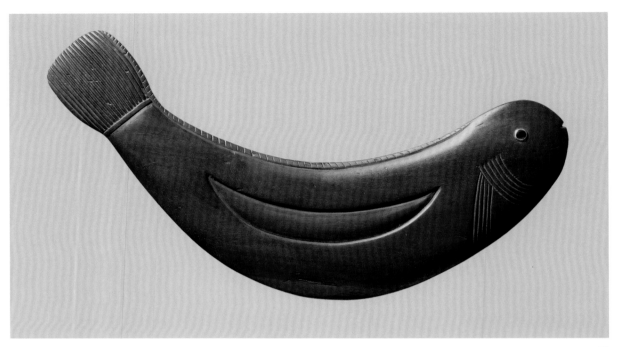

36

feel. The suspension cord of plaited human hair, rarely preserved among surviving examples of *rei miro,* is wrapped around the body of the image for storage, possibly by its original Rapa Nui owner. In contrast with the minimal approach of number 35, number 36 moves in the direction of greater naturalism, transforming the *rei miro* form into the curving body of a fish. Nearly identical to an example collected by H.M.S. *Topaze* in 1868, this image likely dates to the mid-1860s and shows that the island's carving traditions remained strong despite the devastations of the slave trade and introduced disease.

37. Pipe (*puhipuhi*)

19th century
Wood, bone, metal, and pigment; L. 7¼ in. (18.4 cm)
Collection of Mark and Carolyn Blackburn

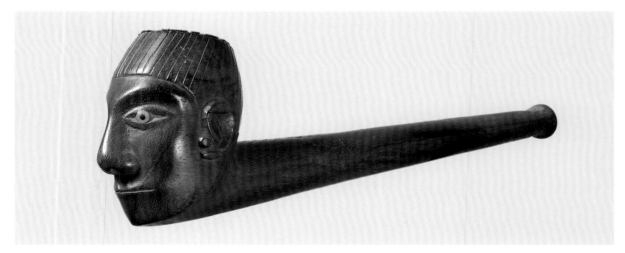

37

68

From the time of first contact, Easter Island artists began to adopt and adapt the materials and objects obtained from passing vessels. Many of the finest Easter Island works incorporate trade items such as red sealing wax, cloth, metal, and imported woods. One of the most appealing examples of this creative interaction between Polynesian art and European objects is this Rapa Nui interpretation of a tobacco pipe.

Tobacco was introduced to the island by European and American sailors in the eighteenth or early nineteenth century. Known on the island as *ava-ava*, it was cultivated from seeds acquired through trade and quickly became popular. In the decades that followed, tobacco became so fully integrated into Rapa Nui culture that some oral traditions recorded in the late nineteenth century assert that it was among the plants brought to the island by the original settlers.[1]

Whether this pipe, which shows evidence of considerable use, was made for local consumption or as a trade item is unclear. Lacking the strong brow ridge, extended earlobes, or goatee characteristic of other anthropomorphic Rapa Nui images, it is possible the pipe depicts a European sailor.

1. Thomson 1891, p. 456; Métraux 1940, p. 64.

38. Barkcloth Headdress (*hau*)

19th century
Reeds, barkcloth, wood, and paint;
L. 12 in. (30.5 cm)
Peabody Museum of Archaeology and Ethnology, Harvard University, Cambridge, Massachusetts; Gift of the Heirs of David Kimball

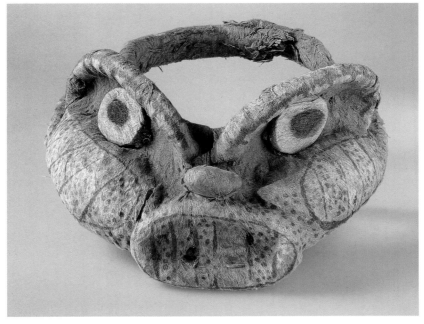

38

The exact function of this headdress, the only surviving example of its type, is unclear. However, its careful modeling, intricately painted surface, and the fact that it incorporates precious barkcloth indicate that it was a highly valuable object probably reserved for important occasions. Worn atop the head like a visor, it likely formed part of the ritual regalia of a chief or priest. Its imagery is similar to the skull-like petroglyphs at Orongo and other sites, which some speculate are images of the god Makemake.[1] If this headdress, by extension, is also a Makemake image, then it might have been worn by individuals portraying the god during the ceremonies of the birdman religion, of which Makemake was the patron deity.[2]

Masks or masklike objects are almost unknown in Polynesia, although some oral traditions indicate they might have existed on Easter Island.[3] An image in the British Museum shows a human wearing what is perhaps a helmetlike bird mask. The birdman image in catalogue number 5 wears what may be interpreted as a visorlike mask depicting a human face, whose form somewhat resembles the present example. If so, this would be a further indication that the barkcloth headdress possibly formed part of the ritual regalia of the birdman religion.

1. Métraux 1940, p. 313.
2. Teilhet 1979, p. 195.
3. Ibid.

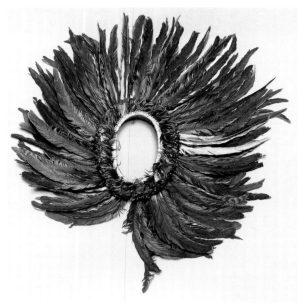

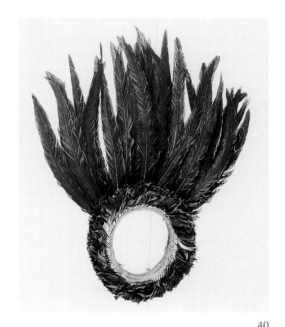

39

40

FEATHER HEADDRESSES

39. Chief's Headddress (*hau hiehie*)

1880s
Feathers and fiber; L. 34⅝ in. (88 cm)
Department of Anthropology, Smithsonian Institution, Washington, D.C.

40. Dance Headddress (*hau vaero*)

1880s
Feathers and fiber; L. 29⅞ in. (76 cm)
Department of Anthropology, Smithsonian Institution, Washington, D.C.

41. Warrior's Headddress (*hau kurakura*)

1880s
Chicken feathers and fiber; L. 16 in. (40.5 cm)
Department of Anthropology, Smithsonian Institution, Washington, D.C.

1. Thomson 1891, p. 518.

Collected in 1886 by an American expedition aboard U.S.S. *Mohican,* these three headdresses are perhaps the finest surviving examples of Rapa Nui featherwork. They are primarily constructed from the highly prized iridescent plumage of domestic roosters but may also include seabird feathers. The most important offering at feasts and ceremonies, chickens were considered sacred, and their feathers were a valuable luxury item. The tail feathers of roosters were held in such esteem that one historical source records chickens with long tails were reserved by victorious chiefs as spoils of war.[1]

As with other types of body ornamentation, feather headdresses were important symbols of an individual's social status. Catalogue numbers 39 and 40 are complex in structure, with a large central cylinder constructed using a false coiling technique in which thin strips of bark were wound around rings of paper mulberry bark or reeds. These rings were then placed on top of one another and bound together with bark string. The feathers were attached to the coils with string so that they projected horizontally.[2]

Surrounded by a shimmering halo of plumes, number 39 is a chief's headdress (*hau hiehie*). It was worn by noble men, and its form and materials embody the power and privileges of chiefly authority. Likely created in the 1880s, the headdress appears to be nearly identical to an example observed in 1774 by Georg Forster, a member of Captain James Cook's expedition. Forster describes an encounter with the Rapa Nui chief "Ko-Toheetai" and notes "on his head he had a cap of long shining black feathers, which might be called a diadem."[3] Such headdresses, worn atop the head with the feathers projecting outward, were often kept in place by a barkcloth strap that passed under the chin.[4]

Catalogue number 40 was identified by its original collector as a dance headdress (*hau vaero*). Adorned with a visorlike line of feathers that likely would have shaded the wearer's face, it is said to have been worn during dance performances and also at marriage feasts.[5] Whether this type of headdress was reserved for dancers of a particular social status is unclear, but the use of highly valued tail feathers suggests it might have been used by members of the nobility.

Adorned with red-orange rooster neck feathers, catalogue number 41 is a warrior's headdress (*hau kurakura*). Literally "headdress of intense red," *hau kurakura* are said to have been worn in combat and also as an item of dance regalia.[6] On Easter Island, as elsewhere in Polynesia, red was considered the most sacred and supernaturally powerful color, and red feathers were rare and precious objects. When worn, the brightly colored feathers of the headdress would have fluttered with a warrior's every movement, giving him a fearsome and intimidating appearance as he ran into battle or danced, perhaps in celebration of victory.[7]

2. Métraux 1940, pp. 221–22.
3. Forster 2000, p. 318.
4. Métraux 1940, p. 222.
5. Thomson 1889, p. 536.
6. Ibid.
7. Geiseler 1883, p. 35.

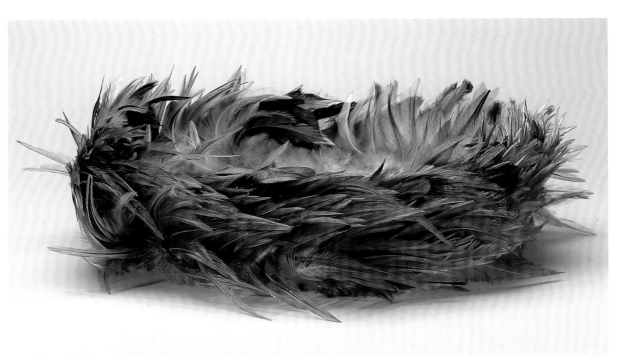

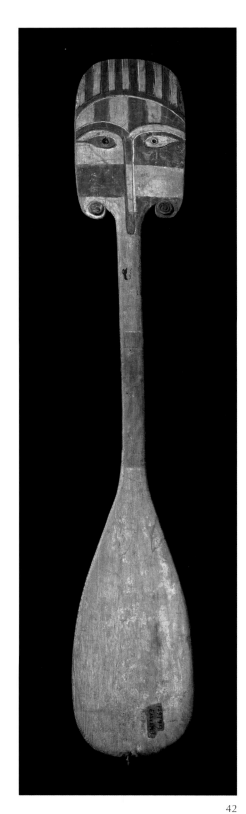

42

1. Routledge 1919, p. 259.
2. Ibid., p. 261.

DANCE PADDLES

42. Dance Paddle ('ao)

1880s
Wood, paint, obsidian, and bone; L. 7 ft. 3¾ in. (222.9 cm)
Department of Anthropology, Smithsonian Institution, Washington, D.C.

Until the mid-nineteenth century, the scale of Rapa Nui wood sculpture was limited by the availability of suitable raw material. This extraordinary dance paddle, carved sometime in the 1880s from an imported plank, offers a rare example of a monumental Rapa Nui work in wood. At more than 7 feet (2.1 m) in length, it is the largest surviving pre-twentieth-century wood image from Easter Island.

Although grand in scale, the work is well within the stylistic canon of the large dance paddles known as 'ao. Usually boldy decorated in red and white pigments obtained from mineralized volcanic tuff, 'ao were used primarily in the dances and ceremonies of the birdman religion.[1] Depictions of 'ao are among the paintings inside the ceremonial dwellings at Orongo, and an enormous 'ao image adorned the interior of the cave on Motu Nui where the chief's champions (*hopu manu*) lived during the ritual egg hunt.[2]

'Ao are essentially more elaborate versions of the smaller dance paddles known as *rapa* (cat. nos. 43, 44). In addition to their greater size, the 'ao generally exhibit a greater emphasis on facial features than is found on the *rapa*. The eyes, as in the example here, occasionally have the distinctive bone and obsidian inlays typical of the small wood images. One 'ao in the Museum für Völkerkunde Vienna also has a fully formed mouth and detailed eyebrows similar to those of *moai kavakava*. The rectilinear designs on the face and forehead of 'ao likely depict face paint patterns. In the context of the birdman religion, the term 'ao denoted both the dance paddles and the ruling elite from whose ranks the birdman was chosen, suggesting that their use was restricted to high chiefs or to dancers performing on their behalf.

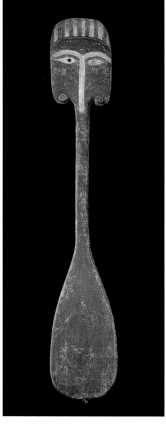

42 (reverse side)

43. Dance Paddle (*rapa*)

19th century
Wood; L. 28¼ in. (71.8 cm)
The Metropolitan Museum of Art, New
York; The Michael C. Rockefeller
Memorial Collection, Gift of Mrs. Gertrud
A. Mellon, 1972
1978.412.1571

44. Dance Paddle (*rapa*)

19th century
Wood; L. 33¼ in. (84.5 cm)
Private collection

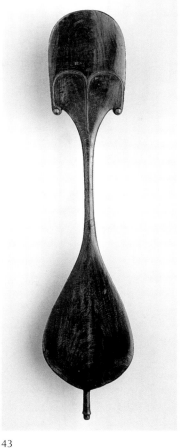

43

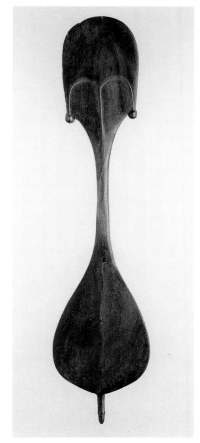

44

Rapa Nui art is especially notable for the tremendous plasticity of its approaches to the human form. Easter Island's small, unpainted dance paddles (*rapa*) push the human image to the limits of abstraction. The paddles represent highly stylized human figures that are reduced to bladelike forms depicting the head and abdomen. The normally detailed facial features of Rapa Nui wood sculpture are here refined into a single curving brow line that incorporates the nose and extends downward at the sides to stylized ear ornaments. The result is an image of the utmost refinement, whose elegant lines make the *rapa* among the most visually striking of the island's diverse wood images.

An essential element of ritual regalia, *rapa* were used in a variety of contexts, from children's dances to funerary rites for slain warriors.[1] They were usually carried in pairs and spun on their axes to the rhythm of a chanted accompaniment.[2] One nineteenth-century source claims the paddles are images of female dancers.[3] While they might have had such female associations, *rapa* were reportedly used by individuals of both sexes, although men and women seldom performed together.[4]

1. Métraux 1940, p. 350; Routledge 1919, p. 229.
2. Métraux 1940, p. 267.
3. Thomson 1891, p. 535. Although the phallic forms attached to the lower abdomen appear to contradict this identification, these appendages actually may depict the artificial elongation of the clitoris (*repe*) formerly practiced by Rapa Nui women. See Métraux 1940, p. 264.
4. Thomson 1891, p. 469.

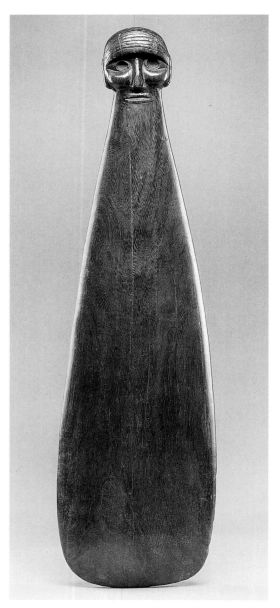

45

45. Club (*paoa*)

18th–19th century
Wood and obsidian; L. 19 in. (48.3 cm)
Private collection

Distinctively Polynesian, the *paoa* of Easter Island share a common origin with the hand clubs (*patu*) of the New Zealand Māori and other groups. Said to have been the preferred weapon among Rapa Nui warriors, *paoa* were used to strike a thrusting blow to the head or ribs during hand-to-hand combat.[1] These short flattened clubs were so intimately linked with their users that Rapa Nui warriors were themselves referred to as *paoa*.[2] The bifacial heads of *paoa* were incorporated into ceremonial objects such as chief's staffs (*ua*; see cat. nos. 46, 47) and the images known as *moai aringa* (see cat. nos. 27–29) possibly as symbols of martial power and prowess. The stylized visual references to *paoa* in these other objects might have identified their owners as warriors (*paoa*) or war leaders (*matatoa*).

This old and deeply patinated *paoa* is at once a functional object and a subtly crafted work of sculpture. With its prominent brow lines, rounded cheeks, and straight, expressionless mouth, it represents the archetypal *moai aringa* image on which the more stylized chief's staffs and pendants are based. As with other *moai aringa*, *paoa* may depict Rau-hiva-aringa-erua, a figure from Rapa Nui mythology.

1. Skinner and Simmons 1974, p. 147.
2. Métraux 1940, p. 138.

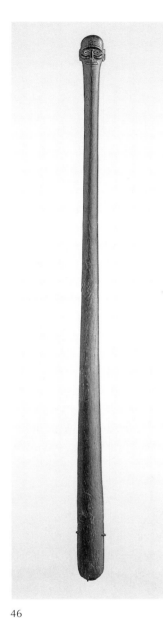

CHIEF'S STAFFS (*ua*)

46. Staff

19th century
Wood, obsidian, and bone; L. 58 in. (147.3 cm)
Helios Trust Collection; courtesy Francesco Pellizzi

47. Staff

19th century
Wood, obsidian, and bone; L. 53⅛ in. (134.9 cm)
Private collection

Among the largest surviving examples of Rapa Nui wood sculpture are the bifacial staffs known as *ua*. Imposing symbols of authority, *ua* were carried by prominent chiefs as marks of their sacred and secular power. Essentially enlarged versions of the hand clubs (*paoa*) used by Rapa Nui warriors (see cat. no. 45), the form of the *ua* may be a symbolic reference to the role of many chiefs as leaders in war (*matatoa*).

Wood was extremely scarce in the late prehistoric and early contact periods, and the long, straight pieces used in the production of *ua* would have been highly valued luxury items reserved for the use of chiefs. Many early examples are slightly crooked or patched with wood plugs,[1] reflecting the great efforts of the artists to overcome the deficiencies in the available raw material and maintain the integrity of the form.

Catalogue number 47 is a classic expression of the *ua* tradition. Its wrinkled brow, stoic countenance, and tablike ears embody the stern, determined image of the chief as *matatoa*. With its unusually delicate, slightly puzzled expression, number 46, by contrast, depicts a lighter, more emotionally accessible variation of the *ua* face. As with the *moai aringa* (see cat. nos. 27–29), the bifacial imagery of the staffs may be a reference to the legendary warrior Rau-hiva-aringa-erua. Historical accounts report that *ua* were individually named, and one source states that the heads represent portraits of their chiefly owners.[2] It is possible, then, that these two *ua*, although highly conventionalized, depict specific individuals.

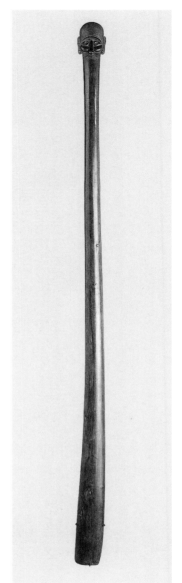

47

1. Métraux 1940, p. 169.
2. Thomson 1891, p. 535; Routledge 1919, p. 268.

46

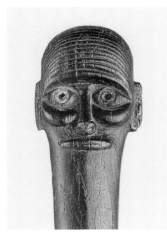

46 (detail)

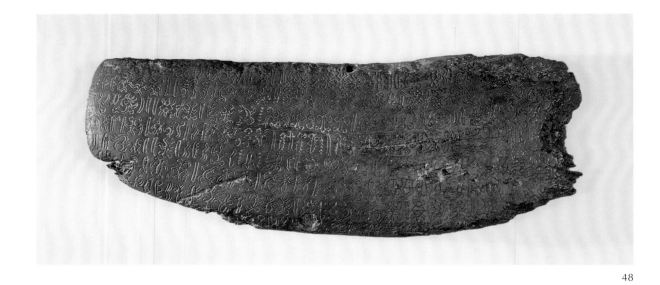

INSCRIBED TABLETS (*kohau rongorongo*)

48. Inscribed Tablet

19th century
Wood; L. 9½ in. (24.1 cm)
Department of Anthropology, Smithsonian Institution, Washington, D.C.

49. Inscribed Tablet

19th century
Wood; L. 24¾ in. (62.9 cm)
Department of Anthropology, Smithsonian Institution, Washington, D.C.

50. Inscribed Tablet

19th century; case, France, early 20th century
Wood; L. 4¼ in. (10.8 cm)
Collection of Mark and Carolyn Blackburn

These three inscribed tablets are among the less than two dozen known examples of Easter Island's unique script (*rongorongo*). The only indigenous script in Oceania, *rongorongo* consists of pictographic symbols that depict anthropomorphs, plants, and geometric motifs as well as objects such as the *rei miro* gorgets worn by chiefly women (see cat. nos. 33–36). Primarily recorded on

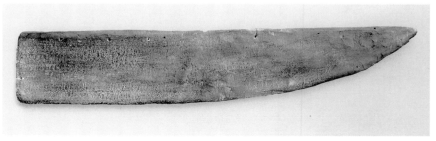

specialized tablets (*kohau rongorongo*), *rongorongo* also appears as shorter inscriptions on some wood objects, including the birdman figure in catalogue number 4. *Rongorongo* was first documented by Catholic missionaries in the 1860s, leading many modern scholars to speculate that it may be a postcontact phenomenon created in imitation of European writing.[1] The script, however, also displays a number of features that argue for an earlier, Rapa Nui origin.[2]

Rongorongo remains one of Oceania's most enduring enigmas. While a number of purported "translations" have been published over the years, none can survive close scrutiny and it remains undeciphered. Even the fundamental nature of the symbols themselves is unclear. It is conceivable that they represent a true writing system in which each symbol stands for a specific sound or word. However, most contemporary scholars believe the individual symbols were simply mnemonic devices designed to help the "reader" remember the contents and order of chants or genealogies without recording the contents themselves.

According to oral tradition, knowledge of *rongorongo* was restricted to a class of priests known as *tangata rongorongo*. Each lineage had one or more *tangata rongorongo*, who reportedly kept separate houses where they met to

1. See Van Tilburg 1994, p. 112.
2. These include the fact that the rows of symbols are alternately inverted, so that after one line has been read, the tablet must be turned upside down to read the next, a feature not seen in any Western script. The symbols also show clear evidence of patterning and, unlike many recorded instances of indigenous imitation of European writing, the individual characters bear no resemblance to Roman letters.

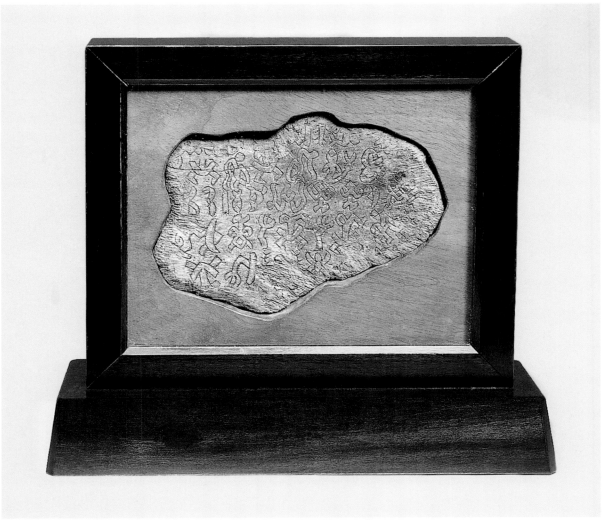

3. Routledge 1919, p. 244.
4. Exactly how many *kohau rongorongo* originally existed is unknown. Some Rapa Nui in the early twentieth century stated that one well-known *tangata rongorongo* had "hundreds" of tablets in his possession and that *kohau rongorongo* could reach lengths of up to 6 feet. Routledge 1919, pp. 244–45. However, the existence of tablets in such large numbers and of such dimensions seems unlikely given the scarcity of wood on the island. Adrienne L. Kaeppler, letter to the author, 2001.
5. Routledge 1919, pp. 248–51.
6. Ibid., p. 207; Thomson 1891, p. 514. Ironically, after initially ordering their destruction, missionaries were later instrumental in saving a number of *kohau rongorongo*.
7. Routledge 1919, p. 207; Thomson 1891, p. 514; Kaeppler, letter to the author, 2001.
8. Fischer 1997, p. 438. To preserve the fragile fragment, Stéphen-Chauvet commissioned its distinctive case from the noted Japanese-born Parisian basemaker Inagaki.

recite with the aid of the tablets and to instruct novices in their use.[3] It is likely that scores of individual tablets originally existed, incorporating diverse aspects of the island's sacred and secular history.[4] Early-twentieth-century sources state that the inscriptions included prayers, ceremonial instructions, and historical records.[5] It is also probable that they recorded myths and chiefly genealogies.

The majority of *tangata rongorongo* were likely among the chiefs and priests captured during the slave raids of 1862–63, and most probably died in Peruvian guano mines and plantations. By the late 1860s, when European scholars first took an interest in the tablets, there were apparently no individuals alive who could still recite from them. In the late nineteenth and early twentieth centuries, Rapa Nui sources reported that many tablets were burned on the order of missionaries, perhaps because of their perceived association with the island's indigenous religion.[6] Other tablets were preserved by being hidden in caves.

Catalogue numbers 48 and 49 were collected in 1886 by U.S.S. *Mohican*. Number 48 is the best preserved and gives an impression of the original appearance of *kohau rongorongo*. Its intricately detailed pictographs display the alternately inverted rows of symbols characteristic of *rongorongo* inscriptions. Number 49, although considerably damaged and worn, still preserves much of its lengthy inscription. It was probably rectangular originally and was later trimmed to its present knifelike shape so that the valuable piece of wood could be reused. According to some late-nineteenth- and early-twentieth-century sources, this tablet was incorporated into a Rapa Nui canoe, but most scholars dismiss this story as apocryphal.[7]

Catalogue number 50 is a partial tablet collected by a French missionary, who sent it to Paris in 1892. Known as the "Chauvet Fragment," it was acquired in 1930 by Parisian collector Charles Stéphen-Chauvet, who included it in his influential book on Easter Island art.[8] Extensively weathered, the piece was likely recovered from a cave. Stéphen-Chauvet went to great lengths to acquire his fragment, and he devoted a substantial section of his book to assembling examples of *kohau rongorongo*. He even provided a detailed, although entirely fanciful, translation of the individual symbols.

gorongo originally existed is

Selected Bibliography

Barthel, Thomas S.

1978 *The Eighth Land: The Polynesian Discovery and Settlement of Easter Island*. Translated from German by Anneliese Martin. Honolulu: University Press of Hawai'i.

Beaglehole, John C., ed.

1961 *The Journals of Captain James Cook on His Voyages of Discovery*. Vol. 2, *The Voyages of the Resolution and Adventure, 1772–1775*. Hakluyt Society Extra Series, no. 35. Cambridge: Cambridge University Press.

Buck, Peter H. (Te Rangi Hiroa)

1938 *Ethnology of Mangareva*. Bernice P. Bishop Museum Bulletin 157. Honolulu.

Bužinska, Irēna

2000 "Some Words about Voldemars Matvejs [Vladimir Markov] and His Book, *The Art of Easter Island*." *Rapa Nui Journal* 14, no. 3, pp. 89–93.

Campbell, Ramón

1987 *La cultura de la Isla de Pascua: Mito y realidad*. Santiago, Chile: Editorial Andrés Bello.

Churchill, William

1912 *Easter Island: The Rapanui Speech and the Peopling of Southeast Polynesia*. Carnegie Institution of Washington, publication no. 174. Washington, D.C.

Cooke, George H.

1899 "Te Pito Te Henua, Known as Rapa Nui, Commonly Called Easter Island, South Pacific Ocean." *United States National Museum, Annual Report for 1897*, pp. 689–723. Washington, D.C.: Smithsonian Institution.

Cristino Ferrando, Claudio, and Patricia Vargas Casanova

1998 "Archaeological Excavations and Restoration at Ahu Tongariki." In Vargas Casanova 1998, pp. 153–58.

Cristino Ferrando, Claudio, Patricia Vargas Casanova, and Roberto Izaurieta San Juan

1981 *Atlas arqueólogica de Isla de Pascua*. Santiago: Universidad de Chile, Facultad de Arquitectura y Urbanismo, Centro de Estudios Isla de Pascua.

Elliot, Robert S.

1979 "Tapa Legacy Update—of Whales and Tapa." *Journal of the New Brunswick Museum*, 1979, pp. 165–68.

Emory, Kenneth P.

1939 *Archaeology of Mangareva and Neighboring Atolls*. Bernice P. Bishop Museum Bulletin 163. Honolulu.

Englert, Sebastián

1948 *La tierra de Hotu Matu'a: Historia, ethnología y lengua de la Isla de Pascua*. [Santiago, Chile]: Editorial San Francisco.

Ferdon, Edwin N., Jr.

1961 "The Ceremonial Site of Orongo." In Heyerdahl and Ferdon 1961, pp. 221–56.

Fischer, Steven R.

1997 *Rongorongo: The Easter Island Script: History, Traditions, Texts*. Oxford: Clarendon Press.

Forster, Georg

1986 *A Voyage round the World*. Revised by Robert L. Kahn. Georg Forsters Werke, vol. 1. Berlin: Akademie-Verlag.

2000 *A Voyage round the World*. Edited by Nicholas Thomas and Oliver Berghof, assisted by Jennifer Newell. Vol. 1. Honolulu: University Press of Hawai'i.

Fuentes, Jordi

1960 *Diccionario y gramática de la lengua de la Isla de Pascua: Pascuense-Castellano, Castellano-Pascuense*. Santiago, Chile: Editorial Andrés Bello.

Geiseler, Wilhelm

1883 *Die Oster-Insel: Eine Stätte prähistorischer Kultur in der Südsee*. Bericht des Kommandanten S.M. Kbt. "Hyäne," Kapitänlieutenant Geiseler, über die ethnologische Untersuchung der Oster-Insel (Rapanui) an den Chef der Kaiserlichen Admiralität. Reprint of *Beiheft zum Marine Verordnungsblatt*, no. 44, pp. 1–54. Berlin: Ernst Sigfried Mittler und Sohn.

Green, Roger C.

1998 "Rapanui Origins Prior to European Contact: The View from Eastern Polynesia." In Vargas Casanova 1998, pp. 87–110.

Green, Roger C., and Marshall I. Weisler

2000 *Mangarevan Archaeology: Interpretations Using New Data and 40 Year Old Excavations to Establish a Sequence from 1200 to 1900 A.D.* University of Otago Studies in Prehistoric Anthropology 19. Dunedin.

Heyerdahl, Thor, and Edwin N. Ferdon Jr., eds.

1961 *Reports of the Norwegian Archaeological Expedition to Easter Island and the East Pacific*. Vol. 1, *Archaeology of Easter Island*. Monographs of the School of American Research and the Museum of New Mexico, no. 24, pt. 1. Santa Fe.

Heyerdahl, Thor, Arne Skjølsvold, and Pavel Pavel

1989 "The 'Walking' Moai of Easter Island." *Kon Tiki Museum Occasional Papers*, no. 1, edited by Arne Skjølsvold, pp. 7–35.

Hotus, Alberto, et al.

1988 *Te Mau Hatu 'o Rapa Nui / Los soberanos de Rapa Nui: Pasado, presente y futuro de Rapa Nui*. [Santiago, Chile]: Editorial Emisión and Centro Latinoamericano Simón Bolívar; in collaboration with the Consejo de Jefes de Rapa Nui.

Kaeppler, Adrienne L.

1982 "Genealogy and Disrespect: A Study of Symbolism in Hawaiian Images." *Res* 3, pp. 82–107.

1984 "Barkcloth Images and Symbolic Continuities in the Arts of Easter Island." Paper presented to the First International Congress on Easter Island and East Polynesia, Hanga Roa, Easter Island.

1989 "Art and Aesthetics." In *Developments in Polynesian Ethnology*, edited by Alan Howard and Robert Borofsky, pp. 211–40. Honolulu: University Press of Hawai'i.

Kirch, Patrick V.

2000 *On the Road of the Winds: An Archaeological History of the Pacific Islands before European Contact*. Berkeley and Los Angeles: University of California Press.

Lee, Georgia

1992 *Rock Art of Easter Island: Symbols of Power, Prayers to the Gods*. Monumenta archaeologica, vol. 17. Los Angeles: [University of California, Los Angeles, Institute of Archaeology].

Martinsson-Wallin, Helene, and Paul Wallin

1998 "Excavations at Anakena: The Easter Island Settlement Sequence and Change of Subsistence?" In Vargas Casanova 1998, pp. 179–86.

Maurer, Evan
1984   "Dada and Surrealism." In Rubin 1984, vol. 2, pp. 535–93.
McCall, Grant
1976   "Reaction to Disaster: Continuity and Change in Rapanui Social Organization." Ph.D. dissertation, Australian National University, Canberra.
Métraux, Alfred
1940   *Ethnology of Easter Island.* Bernice P. Bishop Museum Bulletin 160. Honolulu.
Peltier, Philippe
1984   "From Oceania." In Rubin 1984, vol. 1, pp. 99–124.
Routledge, Katherine Pease
1919   *The Mystery of Easter Island.* London: Sifton, Praed & Co.
1920   "Survey of the Village and Carved Rocks of Orongo, Easter Island, by the Mana Expedition." *Journal of the Royal Anthropological Institute of Great Britain and Ireland* 50, pp. 425–51.
Routledge, Katherine Pease, and W. Scoresby Routledge
n.d.   Papers and correspondence of Katherine and W. Scoresby Routledge concerning their expedition to Easter Island in the yacht *Mana* in 1914–15. Archives of the Royal Geographical Society, London. Copies held at Auckland Public Library, Auckland, New Zealand; Instituto de Estudios Isla de Pascua, Universidad de Chile, Santiago; Pacific Manuscripts Bureau, Canberra, Australia; Rock Art Archive, Cotsen Insitute of Archaeology, University of California, Los Angeles.
Rubin, William, ed.
1984   *"Primitivism" in 20th Century Art: Affinity of the Tribal and the Modern.* 2 vols. Exh. cat. New York: The Museum of Modern Art.
Skinner, Henry D., and David R. Simmons
1974   "Patu in the Pacific." In *Comparatively Speaking: Studies in Pacific Material Culture 1921–1972,* edited by Henry D. Skinner, pp. 147–81. Dunedin: University of Otago Press.
Skjølsvold, Arne
1961   "The Stone Statues and Quarries of Rano Raraku." In Heyerdahl and Ferdon 1961, pp. 339–80.
Stéphen-Chauvet, [Charles]
1935   *L'Île de Pâques et ses mystères: La première étude réunissant tous les documents connus sur cette île mystérieuse.* Éditions "Tel." Paris.
Teilhet, Jehanne H.
1979   "The Equivocal Nature of a Masking Tradition in Polynesia." In *Exploring the Visual Art of Oceania: Australia, Melanesia, Micronesia and Polynesia,* edited by Sidney M. Mead, pp. 192–201. Honolulu: University Press of Hawai'i.
Thomson, William J.
1891   "Te Pito te Henua, or Easter Island." In *United States National Museum, Annual Report for the Year Ending 30 June, 1889,* pp. 447–552. Washington, D.C.: Smithsonian Institution.
Van Tilburg, Jo Anne
1986a   "Power and Symbol: The Stylistic Analysis of Easter Island Monolithic Sculpture." 2 vols. Ph.D. dissertation, University of California, Los Angeles.
1986b   "Red Scoria on Easter Island: Sculpture, Artifacts and Architecture." *Journal of New World Archaeology* 7, no. 1, pp. 1–28.
1987   "Larger Than Life: The Form and Function of Easter Island Monolithic Sculpture." *Musées Royaux d'Art et d'Histoire Bulletin* 58, no. 2, pp. 111–30.
1988   "Stylistic Variation of Dorsal Design on Easter Island Statues." *Clava* (Vina del Mar, Chile: Museo Sociedad Fonck), edited by J. M. Ramírez, 4, pp. 95–108.
1992   *H.M.S.* Topaze *on Easter Island: Hoa Hakananai'a and Five Other Museum Sculptures in Archaeological Context.* British Museum Occasional Paper 73. London.
1994   *Easter Island: Archaeology, Ecology, and Culture.* London: British Museum Press; Washington, D.C.: Smithsonian Institution Press.
1998   "Double Canoes on Easter Island? Reassessing the Orongo Petroglyph Evidence." In Vargas Casanova 1998, pp. 131–46.
Van Tilburg, Jo Anne, and Grant Lee
1987   "Symbolic Stratigraphy: Rock Art and the Monolithic Statues of Easter Island." *World Archaeology* 19, no. 2, pp. 133–45.
Van Tilburg, Jo Anne, and Ted Ralston
1999   "Engineers of Easter Island." *Archaeology* 52, no. 6 (November–December), pp. 40–45.
Van Tilburg, Jo Anne, and Patricia Vargas Casanova
1988   "Transition and Transformation of Easter Island Sculpture: Recent Archaeological Evidence from Ahu O'Pepe." Paper delivered at the Twelfth International Congress of Anthropological and Ethnological Sciences, Zagreb, Yugoslavia, July 28, 30.
1998   "Easter Island Statue Inventory and Documentation: A Status Report." In Vargas Casanova 1998, pp. 187–94.
Vargas Casanova, Patricia, ed.
1998   *Easter Island and East Polynesian Prehistory.* Second International Congress on Easter Island and East Polynesia, Hanga Roa, Easter Island, October 17–21, 1996. Santiago: Universidad de Chile, Facultad de Arquitectura y Urbanismo, Instituto de Estudios Isla de Pascua.
Varnedoe, Kirk
1984   "Gauguin." In Rubin 1984, vol. 1, pp. 179–209.
Weisler, Marshall I.
1998   "Issues in the Colonization and Settlement of Polynesian Islands." In Vargas Casanova 1998, pp. 73–86.

Photograph Credits